hamlyn
QuickCook

hamlyn

QuickCook
Student

Recipes by Jo McAuley

Every dish, three ways – you choose!
30 minutes | 20 minutes | 10 minutes

An Hachette UK Company
www.hachette.co.uk

First published in Great Britain in 2013 by Hamlyn,
a division of Octopus Publishing Group Ltd
Endeavour House, 189 Shaftesbury Avenue
London WC2H 8JY
www.octopusbooks.co.uk

ISBN 978-0-600-62615-2

A CIP catalogue record for this book is available from the British Library.

Printed and bound in China.

10 9 8 7 6 5 4 3 2 1

Both metric and imperial measurements are given for the recipes. Use one set of
measures only, not a mixture of both.

Standard level spoon measurements are used in all recipes

1 tablespoon = 15 ml

1 teaspoon = 5 ml

Ovens should be preheated to the specified temperature. If using a fan-assisted oven,
follow the manufacturer's instructions for adjusting the time and temperature. Grills
should also be preheated.

This book includes dishes made with nuts and nut derivatives. It is advisable for those with
known allergic reactions to nuts and nut derivatives and those who may be potentially
vulnerable to these allergies, such as pregnant and nursing mothers, invalids, the elderly,
babies and children, to avoid dishes made with nuts and nut oils.

It is also prudent to check the labels of pre-prepared ingredients for the possible inclusion
of nut derivatives.

The Department of Health advises that eggs should not be consumed raw. This book
contains some dishes made with raw or lightly cooked eggs. It is prudent for more
vulnerable people such as pregnant and nursing mothers, invalids, the elderly, babies and
young children to avoid uncooked or lightly cooked dishes made with eggs.

Contents

Introduction 6

Breaksfast, Brunch and Lunch 20
Recipes listed by cooking time 22

Brain Food Meals 72
Recipes listed by cooking time 74

Chilled-Out TV Dinners 124
Recipes listed by cooking time 126

Supper for Friends 176
Recipes listed by cooking time 178

Sweet Fix 228
Recipes listed by cooking time 230

Index 280
Acknowledgements 288

Introduction

30 20 10 – Quick, Quicker, Quickest

This book offers a new and flexible approach to meal-planning for busy cooks, letting you choose the recipe option that best fits the time you have available. Inside you will find 360 dishes that will inspire and motivate you to get cooking every day of the year. All the recipes take a maximum of 30 minutes to cook. Some take as little as 20 minutes and, amazingly, many take only 10 minutes. With a bit of preparation, you can easily try out one new recipe from this book each night and slowly you will be able to build a wide and exciting portfolio of recipes to suit your needs.

How Does it Work?

Every recipe in the QuickCook series can be cooked one of three ways – a 30-minute version, a 20-minute version or a super-quick and easy 10-minute version. At the beginning of each chapter you'll find recipes listed by time. Choose a dish based on how much time you have and turn to that page.

You'll find the main recipe in the middle of the page accompanied by a beautiful photograph, as well as two time-variation recipes below.

If you enjoy your chosen dish, why not go back and cook the other time-variation options at a later date? So if you liked the 30-minute Margherita Tart, but only have 10 minutes to spare this time around, you'll find a way to cook it using cheat ingredients or clever shortcuts.

If you love the ingredients and flavours of the 10-minute Citrus Chicken Salad, why not try something more substantial, like the 20-minute Citrus Chicken Couscous, or be inspired to make a more elaborate version, like the Citrus Baked Chicken? Alternatively, browse through all 360 delicious recipes, find something that catches your eye — then cook the version that fits your time frame.

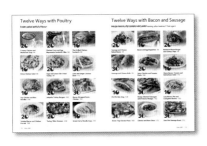

Or, for easy inspiration, turn to the gallery on pages 12–19 to get an instant overview by themes, such as Twelve Ways with Poultry or Twelve Ways with Bacon and Sausage.

STU-BRAI-KAT

QuickCook Online

To make life even easier, you can use the special code on each recipe page to email yourself a recipe card for printing, or email a text-only shopping list to your phone. Go to www.hamlynquickcook.com and enter the recipe code at the bottom of each page.

Student Meals

Becoming a student is not just about academic qualifications. It's also about learning how to survive on your own, which involves learning to cook and manage a tight grocery budget. And while a diet of fast food may seem like the quickest, cheapest, easiest option, it is actually a false economy – it will not satisfy your hunger for as long as a home-cooked meal and can leave you feeling sluggish at best, unwell at worst. Instead, fuel your body for longer with healthy, inexpensive meals. Search through the delicious recipes in this book to find those that tempt you – there are dishes suitable for any occasion, be it a filling supper after sports training or a fun, home-cooked supper with friends, and an entire chapter dedicated to feeding your brain as well as your tummy, using ingredients that are known to aid concentration.

There is no reason why cooking should feel like a chore. The following tips will help you make it more of a pleasure and stretch your budget to provide you with delicious and healthy meals.

Shopping Tips

Skillful shopping will make your pennies go further and keep your belly filled up for longer. Plan your week's meals ahead, then write a list of the ingredients you'll need – and stick to it. It's easy to blow your budget on tempting treats and lavish ingredients without having bought the staples. And avoid walking around a supermarket when you are feeling hungry, which is a recipe for disaster!

Buy dried and canned goods in bulk when you can as it works out cheaper in the long run. Ethnic stores often sell economy size bags of dry produce such as rice and couscous, and may also sell fresh produce more cheaply than supermarkets or greengrocers. Take advantage of supermarket promotions (such as buy-one-get-one-free offers), but only if the produce can be stored for a long time and if you will actually use it (rather than let it rot in the cupboard). Check out local markets towards the end of trading to pick up great bargains. You may need to do some adventurous cooking with whatever ingredients you end with, which is a great opportunity for some kitchen adventures!

Storecupboard Staples

If you always have to hand a supply of useful ingredients, you'll save time on your shopping trips and will always have in the ingredients for at least a few meals that you can knock up. Refer to the list here and stock up with these useful items.

When the funds are running especially low, a few storecupboard essentials can provide you with a super-cheap meal. Although a bowl of pasta with a knob of butter and seasoning is a bit unimaginative, it is a filling emergency standby supper. You'll be surprised how even the cheapest of ingredients can be used to make a fantastic feast when you are hungry and broke.

In the cupboard
- cooking oil (olive, vegetable, sesame)
- canned tomatoes
- canned beans and pulses (cannellini beans, baked beans, kidney beans, chick peas, green lentils)
- canned fish (tuna, mackerel, salmon, sardines, anchovies)
- canned vegetables (potatoes, sweetcorn)
- rice (long-grain, risotto)
- couscous
- pasta (a selection of shapes)
- noodles (rice, egg)
- bulgar wheat
- rolled oats
- dried fruits (ready-to-eat apricots, raisins)
- nuts (walnuts, almonds, hazelnuts)
- sunflower seeds
- flour (plain, self-raising, cornflour)
- baking powder
- vanilla extract
- sugar (caster, soft brown)
- honey
- maple syrup
- golden syrup
- eggs
- garlic
- onions
- potatoes

Herbs, spices and condiments
- salt and pepper
- ground spices (cumin, coriander, cinnamon, ginger)
- paprika
- chilli flakes
- dried herbs (basil, oregano, rosemary, sage, thyme, mixed herbs)
- mustard powder
- wholegrain mustard
- harissa
- Tabasco sauce
- Worcestershire sauce
- sweet chilli sauce
- ketchup
- mayonnaise
- fish sauce
- soy sauce (dark, light)
- stock cubes or concentrates (vegetable, chicken, beef)
- tomato purée
- vinegars (red wine, white wine, balsamic)

In the freezer
- frozen meat and fish (use BOGOF offers)
- frozen vegetables (peas, sweetcorn, leaf spinach)
- puff pastry
- breads (including tortilla wraps, pitta bread)

In the refrigerator
- butter
- milk
- natural yogurt
- cheese (Cheddar cheese, hard Italian cheese such as Grana Padano or Parmesan)
- fresh herbs (coriander, parsley, chives, mint, basil)
- fresh chillies
- fresh root ginger
- lemons
- celery
- carrots
- spring onions
- bacon
- chorizo

Learning to Cheat

There are things you can do to make life easier for yourself in the kitchen. For example, cook larger-than-needed portions and eat the same meal for two days in a row to avoid cooking every day. Or transform the remainder into a new meal with a bit of thought and some useful storecupboard staples. For instance, if you have leftover beef and tomato sauce for pasta, add a few shakes of Tabasco sauce and a can of red kidney beans and serve a chilli the next day.

You don't always have to follow a recipe, either. Having a few reliable fall-back suppers should stop you reaching for that delivery pizza menu. For example, bake a potato and fill it with canned tuna, tomato and cheese or hot baked beans for a quick, filling and nutritious meal. Or make a quick, simple tomato sauce, then add whatever you have in the refrigerator or cupboard (such as chopped ham, mushrooms or a pinch of chilli flakes) to liven it up and serve it with pasta. Or use leftover veggies to make a hearty bowl of soup – fry them gently, then top up the pan with hot water and a stock cube and simmer until tender. Once tender, blend until smooth or ladle into bowls as a chunky soup. And remember – if you have eggs, you have a meal, whether it's a comforting hard-boiled egg with soldiers, a fried egg on toast or a simple cheese omelette.

Healthy Eating

There are many small choices you can make to eat for good health. For example, even if time is precious, don't skip breakfast. Make a fruit-filled smoothie to fuel your body for the coming day and tick off a few of your five-a-day early on. Add some frozen vegetables to a pasta sauce to boost your veggie intake, and stir a can of sweetcorn into the tuna mayonnaise you're making. Snack on fresh or dried fruits rather than biscuits or crisps. To pad out a meal, use cans of drained beans or pulses. Choose wholewheat pasta and brown rice. Also, use a wide variety of fresh fruits and vegetables, meats and fish to keep your diet rich in a range of nutrients.

Store fresh fruit and vegetables correctly and eat them as soon as possible after purchasing to maximise the amount of nutrients you get from them. Vary cooking methods to include poaching, grilling or baking. Avoid frying to reduce your fat intake, and buy leaner cuts of meat. If only curry or pizza will do, try making your own. It will be lower in fat and salt and taste better than "the real thing". Ready-made curry pastes often have simple recipes on the back of the jar, and you can buy decent ready-made pizza bases or mixes if you don't feel like making your own. Make it healthy by adding a colourful array of veggie toppings.

Hygiene in the Kitchen

Use common sense and follow a few simple guidelines to avoid food-poisoning. Ensure your refrigerator is in good working order and that the temperature is correct (you can buy a special refrigerator thermometer cheaply). Pack away chilled and frozen goods as soon as you get home from shopping. Rotate the contents of the refrigerator so that foods closest to their expiry dates are used up first.

Store raw meat and fish on the bottom shelf of the refrigerator, away from other foods, and keep vegetables in the salad drawer (which is designed for this use). Use airtight containers for storing leftovers, or cover them with clingfilm.

Add refrigerator cleaning to any cleaning rota you have going in your house – it may look clean, but a refrigerator can be the ideal place for lurking bacteria to multiply. The same can be said for the kitchen itself and worktop surfaces. Empty bins, clean the oven, sweep the floor and wipe worktops to keep the kitchen clean and tidy and a place in which you will enjoy preparing food.

Have Fun!

Student life is supposed to be fun, and there is no need for shopping, preparation and cooking to become a chore. Invite your friends round to help you prepare and enjoy some meals and you'll have friends for life – as well as many return invitations. Vary recipes as much as possible and be adventurous. Cooking could become a passion! Experiment, have fun in the kitchen, enjoy some great home-cooked meals and hone a few skills – then take these skills home to impress your family during the holidays!

Twelve Ways with Poultry

Protein-packed and full of flavour.

Creamy Chicken and Mushroom Soup 44

Chicken Cress and Egg Mayonnaise Sandwich-Filler 60

Thai Grilled Chicken Sandwich 68

Citrus Chicken Salad 80

Sage and Lemon Stir-Fried Turkey 98

Lime and Ginger Chicken Bowl 112

Soy Chicken and Rice Noodles 146

Jalepeño Turkey Burgers 162

Bacon-Wrapped Pesto Chicken 192

Smoked Bacon and Chicken Parcels 198

Turkey Tikka Skewers 204

Green Curry Noodle Soup 218

Twelve Ways with Bacon and Sausage

Thought these fry-up stalwarts were just for morning-after brekkies? Think again!

Sausage and Cheese Baked Beans 34

Bacon and Egg Baguettes 36

Barbecue Bacon Burger and Cheesy Chips 56

Sausage and Cheese Rolls 70

Spicy Chorizo and Tomato Pasta 104

Warm Bacon, Tomato and Butter Bean Salad 110

Piri Piri Hot-Dog 128

Honey-Mustard Sausages with Polenta Wedges 142

Lazy Bacon, Pea and Courgette Risotto 150

Stove-Top Chorizo Pizza 160

Chorizo and Bean Stew 172

One-Pan Sausage Roast 212

Brain Boosters

Get the grey matter working with these Omega-rich delights.

1 Skint Smoked Salmon and
Cream Cheese Bagel 42

1 Smoked Salmon and Chive
Mayonnaise 64

2 Herby Pan-Fried Salmon 76

1 Flaked Mackerel and
Pepper Couscous 86

3 Sweet Chilli Salmon
Fishcakes 92

1 Sardine and Three-Bean
Salad 102

3 Beetroot, Mackerel and
Goats' Cheese Lentils 114

2 Warm Sardine, Bean and
Potato Salad 116

3 Lemony Salmon Goujons 122

1 Teriyaki Salmon Noodles 180

1 Flaked Mackerel Salad with
Lemon Dressing 202

1 Fisherman's Sardine and
Potato Salad 226

Veggie Delights

The easy way to your 5-a-day – your mum will be so proud.

Leek and Mushroom Pasty 40

Chilli Corn Fritters 46

Mushroom and Onion Tartlets 50

Vegetable Pasta Bowl 82

Healthy Green Bean and Broccoli Salad 96

Red Cabbage and Beetroot Lentils 108

Steamed Bulgar with Grilled Vegetables 138

Green Pepper and Mushroom Stroganoff 190

Margherita Tart 206

Roasted Peppers with Mozzarella and Couscous 220

Gingery Grilled Tofu with Noodles 222

Vegetable Curry with Sticky Rice 224

One-Pot Wonders

One pot = less washing-up. Simple.

French Onion Soup with Cheesy Croûtons 52

Sizzling Beef and Broccoli Stir-Fry 78

Beef and Potato Balti with Spinach 84

Red Pepper, Kidney Bean and Spinach Stew 90

Spiced Vegetable and Chickpea Soup 94

Quick Garlicky Tomato Lentils 132

Creamy Fish Pie 136

Chunky Spiced Bean Soup 140

Creamy Curried Prawns 210

Frozen Fruit Pudding 252

Fresh Fruit Salad 268

Sweet and Sticky Raisin Pudding 276

Cheap Eats

Can't face another meal of beans on toast? Salvation is here.

Apricot and Prune Muesli 24

Corned Beef Hash 48

Quick Cauliflower Cheese 54

Grilled Harissa Lamb Pittas 88

Tuna and Olive Pasta 130

Potato, Cauliflower and Spinach Curry 148

Lemon Butter Fried Fish 156

Tomato and Basil Soup 182

Barbecue Pork Steaks with Corn and Rice 208

Vanilla and Raspberry Fairy Cakes 236

Chewy Oat and Raisin Bars 248

Chocolate Buttermilk Pancakes 254

Pasta, Noodles and Rice

Filling, tasty and great for feeding a crowd.

20

Tuna and Chive Rice Salad 58

30

Wholewheat Pasta Bake with Blue Cheese and Walnuts 100

20

Carrot and Broccoli Vegetable Stir-Fry 106

30

Spaghetti and Meatballs with Spicy Tomato Sauce 120

10

Mushroom and Egg-Fried Rice 134

10

Quick-Cook Pasta with Chillies and Anchovies 152

20

Tuna Gnocchi Bake 154

10

Veggie Noodle Salad 164

10

Chilli Pea Pasta 166

10

Spaghetti with Garlic and Black Pepper 170

20

Poor Man's Pesto with Penne 196

30

Creamy Mushroom and Chive Risotto 214

Hangover Helpers

For days when a little extra help is needed...

Honeyed Granola Pancakes 26

Blueberry and Maple Smoothie 28

Spicy Peanut and Beef Wrap 118

Cheese and Onion Potato Waffles 144

Sweet and Sour Pork 168

Beef and Onion Wraps 174

Mexican Chilli Beef Burger 184

Spiced Lamb Kebab with Couscous 186

Breaded Fish with Mushy Peas 216

Chocolate Orange Cheesecake 240

Stewed Rhubarb with Custard 250

Lemon Popping Candy Cakes 262

QuickCook

Breakfast, Brunch and Lunch

Recipes listed by cooking time

30

Bircher-Style Muesli with Apricots and Prunes 24

Great Granola 26

Blueberry Maple Breakfast Muffin 28

Banana and Bran Muffins 30

Quick Baked Ham and Egg 32

One-Pan Sausage Fry-Up 34

Bacon and Cheese Spanish Omelette 36

Spicy Brunch Enchiladas 38

Leek and Mushroom Pasty 40

Skint Smoked Salmon and Herb Tart 42

Creamy Chicken and Mushroom Pie 44

Chilli Corn Muffins 46

Corned Beef Hash 48

Leek, Mustard and Onion Tart 50

French Onion Soup with Cheesy Croûtons 52

Potato and Cauliflower Soup 54

Barbecue Pork Strips 56

Tuna, Chive and Potato Gratin 58

Chicken, Cress and Onion Sandwich Filler 60

Bean and Parsley Stew 62

Canned Salmon and Chive Fishcakes 64

Carrot and Feta Potato Cakes 66

Thai Curry Rice Bowl 68

Sausage and Cheese Rolls 70

20

Proper Porridge with Apricots and Prunes 24

Honeyed Granola Pancakes 26

Blueberry Maple Pancakes 28

Baked Banana and Bran Porridge 30

Quick Ham and Egg Tortilla 32

Sausage and Cheese Baked Beans 34

Bacon, Egg and Cheese Panini 36

Spicy Brunch Burritos 38

Leek and Mushroom Frittata 40

Skint Smoked Salmon Scramble 42

Creamy Chicken and Mushroom Soup 44

Chilli Corn Fritters 46

Corned Beef Fritters 48

Mustard and Onion Tartlets 50

Cheese and Onion Croque Madame 52

Quick Cauliflower Cheese 54

10

Barbecue Bacon Burger and Cheesy Chips 56

Tuna and Chive Rice Salad 58

Chicken, Cress and Egg Mayonnaise Sandwich Filler 60

Bean and Parsley Patties 62

Fresh Salmon and Chive Burgers 64

Carrot and Feta Bubble and Squeak 66

Thai Curry Noodle Soup 68

Sausage and Cheese Fold-Over 70

Apricot and Prune Muesli 24

Honeyed Granola Yogurt 26

Blueberry and Maple Smoothie 28

Banana and Jam Toasts 30

Quick Ham and Eggs Benedict 32

Sausage and Egg Scramble 34

Bacon and Egg Baguette 36

Spicy Brunch Quesadillas 38

Buttery Leek and Mushrooms on Toast 40

Skint Smoked Salmon and Cream Cheese Bagel 42

Creamy Grilled Mushrooms 44

Chilli Corn Cheese Muffins 46

Corned Beef and Onion Bagel 48

Mustard and Onion Melts 50

Cheese and Onion Toasted Sandwich 52

Creamy Cauliflower Coleslaw 54

Barbecue Bacon Bagel 56

Grilled Tuna and Chive Melts 58

Tandoori Chicken and Cress Sandwich Filler 60

Bean and Parsley Pâté 62

Smoked Salmon and Chive Mayonnaise 64

Feta and Parsley Dip with Carrot Sticks 66

Thai Grilled Chicken Sandwich 68

Grilled Sausage and Cheese Rarebit 70

1 Apricot and Prune Muesli

Serves 4

75 g (3 oz) whole hazelnuts

75 g (3 oz) rolled oats

75 g (3 oz) Bran Flakes, All-Bran or similar bran-based breakfast cereal

2 tablespoons sunflower or mixed seeds (optional)

75 g (3 oz) ready-to-eat dried apricots, sliced

50 g (3 oz) ready-to-eat dried prunes, chopped

To serve

milk and honey

sliced banana or apple (optional)

- Place the hazelnuts in a small, dry frying pan and heat gently for 4–5 minutes, shaking the pan occasionally, until lightly toasted. Tip into the bowl of a mortar, crush lightly with a pestle and set aside to cool.

- Meanwhile, combine the oats, Bran Flakes or All-Bran, seeds and dried fruits. Add the toasted hazelnuts, then divide between 4 bowls and serve immediately with milk and honey and sliced banana or apple, if desired. Alternatively, double the recipe and store for up to a week in an airtight container.

---

2 Proper Porridge with Apricots and Prunes

Place 100 g (3½ oz) each of sliced dried apricots and prunes in a small pan with 100 ml (3½ fl oz) apple juice, ¼ teaspoon ground cinnamon and 2 tablespoons runny honey. Simmer gently for 8–10 minutes until the fruit is tender and syrupy. Set aside to cool slightly. Meanwhile, place 150 g (4 oz) porridge oats in a medium-sized saucepan with 1 litre (1¾ pints) milk and a pinch of salt. Place over a medium heat and bring to the boil, stirring frequently. Reduce the heat and simmer gently for 12–15 minutes until the oats are cooked and the porridge is creamy. Spoon into bowls and serve topped with the syrupy fruit.

3 Bircher-Style Muesli with Apricots and Prunes

In a bowl, combine 325 g (11 oz) of your preferred muesli with 300 ml (½ pint) apple juice, 200 g (7 oz) natural yogurt, 200 ml (7 fl oz) milk, 2 tablespoons honey and 50 g (2 oz) each of chopped dried apricots and prunes. Cover and set aside for at least 25 minutes or, alternatively, cover and refrigerate overnight for the following morning. Serve with slices of fresh banana or apple.

STU-BREA-GIG

 Honeyed Granola Pancakes

Serves 4

150 g (5 oz) plain flour
2 teaspoons baking powder
2 eggs
275 ml (9 fl oz) milk
3 tablespoons clear honey
200 g (7 oz) crunchy, granola-
    style cereal, lightly crushed
50 g (2 oz) butter

To serve

clear honey
Greek yogurt (optional)

- Sift the flour and baking powder together into a large bowl, then make a well in the centre of the mixture. Whisk together the eggs, milk and honey and pour into the well. Whisk the wet ingredients in the well as you gradually incorporate the flour into the mixture. Stir in the granola.

- Melt a knob of butter in a large non-stick frying pan and pour small amounts of the batter into the pan to form small, thick pancakes that are about 8 cm (3¼ inches) in diameter. Cook over a medium-low heat for 2–3 minutes until bubbles start appearing on the surface of the pancakes. Flip over and cook the other side for a further minute, until golden. Repeat with the remaining mixture until you have made all the pancakes. (This quantity of batter should yield about 16 pancakes.)

- Arrange the pancakes on warmed serving plates and serve immediately with a drizzle of honey and a dollop of Greek yogurt, if desired.

Honeyed Granola Yogurt

Spoon 1 tablespoon clear honey into the bottom of 4 glass tumblers. Divide 400 g (13 oz) natural or Greek yogurt between the tumblers and top each one with 2–3 tablespoons of granola. Serve immediately.

Great Granola

Melt 4 tablespoons honey with 50 g (2 oz) butter in a large pan and stir in 200 g (7 oz) porridge oats, 50 g (2 oz) chopped nuts, 50 g (2 oz) mixed or sunflower seeds and ½ teaspoon ground cinnamon or ginger (optional). Tip evenly onto a large baking sheet and bake in a preheated oven, 160°C (325°F), Gas Mark 3, for 15–20 minutes until pale golden, turning once. Remove from the oven and allow to cool slightly, then stir in 75 g (3 oz) raisins. Serve with milk or yogurt. Store in an airtight container for about 1 week.

STU-BREA-PIM

10 Blueberry and Maple Smoothie

Serves 6

6 bananas

3 small handfuls of blueberries

150 g (5 oz) fruit-and-nut muesli

600 g (1 lb 3½ oz) plain or fruit
  yogurt

750 ml (1¼ pint) milk

3–6 tablespoons maple syrup
  or honey

- Place 2 bananas and a small handful of blueberries in the jug of a blender and add a third of the muesli, 200 g (7 oz) yogurt, 250 ml (8 fl oz) milk and 1–2 tablespoons honey or maple syrup. Blend until smooth but thick, then pour into 2 tall glasses to serve. Repeat twice more to make 4 more smoothies.

- Alternatively, if you do not own a blender, pour the muesli into 6 bowls, spoon over the yogurt and top with the sliced banana. Scatter over the blueberries, drizzle over the honey or maple syrup and serve with spoons as a filling breakfast.

20 Blueberry Maple Pancakes

In a bowl, mix 225 g (7½ oz) sifted self-raising flour with 2 teaspoons baking powder and make a slight dip in the centre. Add 1 large lightly beaten egg, 1 tablespoon melted butter and 300 ml (½ pint) buttermilk and whisk until smooth and thick. Stir in 75 g (3 oz) fresh or frozen blueberries. Melt 25 g (1 oz) butter in a non-stick frying pan and pour 3–4 large tablespoons of the batter into the pan. Cook gently for 2–3 minutes until bubbles begin to appear on the surface of the pancakes, then carefully flip them over and cook for a further minute until golden. Remove and keep warm while you repeat the process to use up the remaining batter (this quantity yields about 12 pancakes). To serve, top with rashers or crispy bacon, if desired, and drizzle with warmed maple syrup.

30 Blueberry Maple Breakfast Muffin

In a large bowl, mix 200 g (7 oz) plain flour, 75 g (3 oz) caster sugar, 2 teaspoons baking powder, ½ teaspoon vanilla extract (optional) and 4 tablespoons muesli. Whisk 75 ml (3 fl oz) vegetable oil with 200 ml (7 fl oz) natural yogurt and 2 eggs and pour into the bowl with 100 g (3½ oz) blueberries. Stir until barely combined. Divide between the greased or paper case-lined cups of a 12-cup muffin tin and bake in a preheated oven, 180°C (350°F), Gas Mark 4, for 18–20 minutes. Serve warm, drizzled with maple syrup.

STU-BREA-VAF

3⦿ Banana and Bran Muffins

Serves 4

50 g (2 oz) banana chips, crushed
200 g (7 oz) plain flour
2 teaspoons baking powder
½ teaspoon ground cinnamon
  (optional)
50 g (2 oz) dark soft brown
  or caster sugar
25 g (1 oz) bran or crushed
  All-Bran
2 eggs
50 g (2 oz) butter, melted
125 ml (4 fl oz) buttermilk
1 ripe banana, mashed

- Place the banana chips in a large bowl with the remaining dry ingredients. Whisk together all the remaining ingredients in a jug.

- Pour the wet ingredients into the dry ingredients and stir until barely combined. Divide the mixture between the greased or paper case-lined cups of a 12-cup muffin tin and bake in a preheated oven, 180°C (350°F), Gas Mark 4, for 18–22 minutes until risen and firm to the touch. Transfer to wire racks to cool slightly and serve warm.

1⦿ Banana and Jam Toasts

Toast and butter 4 thick slices of granary or brown bread. In a bowl, mash 2 ripe bananas with ¼ teaspoon ground cinnamon and 2 teaspoons runny honey. Spread this mixture thickly over the slices of buttered toast and top each one with a heaped teaspoon of your preferred fruit jam. Serve with glasses of orange juice and a small pot of yogurt for a healthy, balanced breakfast.

2⦿ Baked Banana and Bran Porridge

Wrap 4 bananas in kitchen foil and bake in a preheated oven, 180°C (350°F), Gas Mark 4, for 10–15 minutes until the skins are blackened and the flesh has softened. Meanwhile, place 125 g (4 oz) porridge oats in a medium-sized saucepan with 50 g (2 oz) bran, 1 litre (1¾ pints) milk, a pinch of salt and ½ teaspoon ground cinnamon (optional). Place over a medium heat and bring

to the boil, stirring frequently. Reduce the heat and simmer gently for 12–15 minutes, stirring frequently, until the oats are cooked and the porridge is creamy. Scrape the flesh of the bananas into the pan and stir into the hot porridge. Spoon into bowls and sprinkle with a teaspoon of soft brown sugar to serve, if desired.

1⏱ Quick Ham and Eggs Benedict

Serves 2

2 teaspoons white vinegar
(such white wine, cider
or malt vinegar)
4 eggs
15 g (½ oz) butter
15 g (½ oz) packet powdered
Hollandaise sauce mix
150 ml (¼ pint) milk
2 English muffins, split
150 g (5 oz) wafer-thin ham
pepper

- Bring a large pan of water to a gentle simmer and add the vinegar. Stir the water with a large spoon to create a swirl and carefully crack an egg into the water, followed by a second. Cook for 3 minutes, then remove with a slotted spoon and keep warm. Repeat the process with the remaining eggs.

- Meanwhile, melt the butter in a small saucepan and stir in the Hollandaise mix. Slowly pour in the milk, stirring to prevent lumps from forming. Bring to the boil, then reduce the heat and simmer gently for 1–2 minutes. (Alternatively, make up the Hollandaise sauce according to the packet instructions.)

- Lightly toast the muffins and arrange on serving plates. Top each muffin half with some wafer-thin ham. Place 1 poached egg on top of each muffin half and spoon over some sauce. Season with pepper and serve immediately.

2⏱ Quick Ham and Egg Tortilla

Melt 25 g (1 oz) butter in a frying pan and cook 3 thinly sliced spring onions over a medium heat for 3–4 minutes until softened. Meanwhile, beat 5 eggs with a pinch each of salt and pepper. Add 100 g (3½ oz) drained and sliced roasted red pepper, 200 g (7 oz) chopped ham and 1 tablespoon chopped chives (optional). Pour into the pan and cook gently for 4–5 minutes until almost set. Crumble over 125 g (4 oz) goats' cheese or feta and cook under a preheated medium-high grill for 2–3 minutes until golden. Cool slightly, then serve in wedges.

3⏱ Quick Baked Ham and Egg

Heat 25 g (1 oz) butter in a large frying pan and cook 3 thinly sliced spring onions over a medium heat for 3–4 minutes until softened. Add 125 g (4 oz) washed spinach leaves and stir for 1–2 minutes until wilted. Remove from the heat and mix with 200 g (7 oz) chopped ham and 1 tablespoon chopped chives or parsley (optional). Scrape the mixture into a buttered shallow ovenproof dish, then carefully crack 4 small eggs over the top. Drizzle 100 ml (3½ fl oz) double cream over the eggs, sprinkle with grated Parmesan cheese or other hard Italian cheese and bake in a preheated oven, 200°C (400°F), Gas Mark 6, for 15–20 minutes until the eggs are just set but still creamy. Remove from the oven and serve with plenty of crusty bread. (Alternatively, divide the mixture between 2 individual dishes or shallow ramekins and cook for 10–15 minutes until just set but still creamy.)

STU-BREA-WUH

Sausage and Cheese Baked Beans

Serves 2

4 herby farmhouse sausages

1 tablespoon vegetable oil

1 garlic clove, crushed

1 teaspoon paprika (optional)

1 teaspoon onion powder or granules (optional)

400 g (13 oz) can haricot beans, rinsed and drained

350 g (11½ oz) passata or sieved tomatoes

1 teaspoon Worcestershire sauce

1 teaspoon dark brown sugar or black treacle

2–4 slices of your preferred bread

butter, for spreading

100 g (3½ oz) grated Cheddar cheese

- Arrange the sausages on the rack of a foil-lined grill tray and slide the tray under a grill preheated to a medium setting. Grill the sausages for about 15 minutes, turning occasionally, until cooked through and golden. Remove and keep warm.

- While the sausages are cooking, heat the oil in a saucepan and cook the garlic gently for 1 minute before adding the paprika. Cook for a further minute, then add the onion powder or granules, beans, passata or sieved tomatoes, Worcestershire sauce and sugar or treacle. Simmer gently for about 15 minutes until the beans are soft and the sauce has thickened slightly.

- Towards the end of the cooking time for the beans and sausages, toast and butter the slices of bread.

- Slice the sausages thickly, then combine with the beans. According to preference, either stir the cheese into the mixture, then spoon it onto the slices of buttered toast, or spoon the beans-and-sausage mixture onto the slices of buttered toast and sprinkle over the grated cheese.

 Sausage and Egg Scramble

Beat 4 eggs with 3 tablespoons milk and a pinch of salt and pepper. Melt 25 g (1 oz) butter in a non-stick pan. Pour in the eggs. When they begin to set, stir gently over a low heat for 3–4 minutes until just set. Stir in 4 thinly sliced Frankfurters or cooked sausages and heat gently until the eggs are lightly set but creamy and the sausages are warmed through. Spoon onto hot buttered toast to serve.

 One-Pan Sausage Fry-Up

Heat 2 tablespoons vegetable oil in a large non-stick frying pan and add 4 thin pork sausages. Cook over medium heat, turning occasionally, for 10–12 minutes until cooked through. Remove from the pan and set aside. Add 4 slices of back bacon and fry over a medium heat for 2–3 minutes on each side until crisp and golden. Remove from the pan and set aside. Tip 200 g (7 oz) thickly sliced mushrooms into the pan and cook over a medium heat for 4–5 minutes, turning occasionally, until softened and lightly golden. Return the meats to the pan and arrange so that you have equal amounts on each side of the pan. Crack 1 egg into each half of the pan and cook gently for 3–5 minutes, depending on how well done you like your eggs. Use a fish slice to lift the cooked breakfasts onto 2 plates and serve with lots of buttered toast.

STU-BREA-CYY

Bacon and Egg Baguette

Serves 2

25 g (1 oz) butter or margarine
3 eggs
1 tablespoon chopped chives
6 slices of rindless streaky bacon
2 individual sandwich baguettes
your preferred sauce (such as
   ketchup, brown sauce, barbecue
   sauce or mayonnaise)
2 small handfuls of rocket or baby
   spinach (optional)
salt and pepper

- Melt the butter gently in a large frying pan while you beat the eggs with the chives and seasoning in a small bowl. Pour the egg mixture into the pan and swirl to cover the base of the pan. Cook over a medium heat for 2–3 minutes until the base is golden. Flip over and cook for a further 2 minutes or until the egg is set and both sides are golden. Remove from the pan, cool slightly, then cut into slices.

- While the egg is cooking, arrange the bacon on the rack of a foil-lined grill tray and cook under a grill preheated to a medium setting for 4–5 minutes until crisp and golden.

- Slice open the baguettes and spread with your preferred sauce before topping with the egg, bacon and rocket or spinach leaves, if using. Serve immediately.

2 Bacon, Egg and Cheese Panini

Heat 1 tablespoon vegetable oil in a frying pan and cook 6 slices of rindless streaky bacon over a medium heat for 4–5 minutes, turning once, until crisp and golden. (Alternatively, arrange the bacon on the rack of a foil-lined grill tray and cook under a grill preheated to a medium setting for the same amount of time.) Remove the bacon and drain on kitchen paper. Split open 2 large bread rolls and spread each roll with 2 teaspoons wholegrain mustard or your preferred sauce. Fill the rolls with the crispy bacon and top with 100 g (3½ oz) sliced Double Gloucester or Cheddar cheese, then scatter ½ thinly sliced red onion over the cheese, if desired, and close. Heat a dry frying pan and place the rolls in the pan. Weight them down by resting a saucepan on top and toast over a medium-low heat for 2–3 minutes until crisp and golden. Flip over and toast the other side for a further 2–3 minutes until the rolls are toasted and the cheese is melting. Meanwhile, crack 2 eggs into the pan, adding a little oil, if necessary, and cook over a medium heat for 3–4 minutes until the eggs are cooked to your liking. Remove the paninis from the pan and serve each one topped with a fried egg.

3 Bacon and Cheese Spanish Omelette

Heat 1 tablespoon oil in a frying pan with a knob of butter and cook 4 chopped slices of bacon over a medium heat for 5–6 minutes. Add 1 sliced onion and cook for 7–8 minutes until softened. Meanwhile, beat 3 eggs with 1 tablespoon chopped chives and a pinch each of salt and pepper. Reduce the heat, stir the eggs into the pan and cook gently for 4–5 minutes until almost set. Sprinkle over 100 g (3½ oz) grated Cheddar cheese and transfer to a medium grill for 4–5 minutes until the egg has set and the topping is golden. Cut into wedges to serve.

Spicy Brunch Quesadillas

Serves 2

200 g (7 oz) can refried beans
4 plain tortilla wraps
1 small avocado, stoned, peeled
  and diced
2 tomatoes, diced
125 g (4 oz) sliced mozzarella
  or grated Cheddar cheese
shredded Iceberg lettuce
  (optional), to serve

- Spread the refried beans over 2 of the tortillas, then scatter over the avocado and tomato. Scatter with the mozzarella or grated Cheddar, then top each with another tortilla.

- Heat a large frying pan and toast 1 of the quesadillas for 1–2 minutes over a medium heat before flipping it over to toast the other side. Repeat with the second quesadilla. Serve in wedges with shredded lettuce, if desired.

2 Spicy Brunch Burritos

Heat 2 tablespoons vegetable oil in a frying pan and cook 1 sliced onion over a medium heat for 6–7 minutes until softened. Add 200 g (7 oz) thickly sliced mushrooms and cook for 4–5 minutes. Stir in 100 g (3½ oz) drained sweetcorn and 4 sliced Frankfurters and heat gently for 1–2 minutes until hot. (Alternatively, for a vegetarian dish, use a 210 g/7¹/₃ oz can drained chickpeas in place of the sausages.) Spoon the filling onto 4 plain tortilla wraps and top each with 1 tablespoon spicy tomato salsa and a few drops of Tabasco sauce for extra heat. Scatter over 75 g (3 oz) diced or grated mozzarella and roll up each tortilla. Serve hot.

3 Spicy Brunch Enchiladas

In a bowl, combine 100 g (3½ oz) of drained sweetcorn with 2 thinly sliced spring onions, 210 g (7¹/₃ oz) can drained chickpeas, half of a 125 g (4 oz) ball of mozzarella, diced, and half of a 375–400 g (12–13 oz) jar of Mexican cooking sauce (such as enchilada or fajita sauce or paste) or half of a 400 g (13 oz) can chopped tomatoes. Spoon the filling into 4 plain tortilla wraps, then roll tightly and arrange snugly in an ovenproof dish. Pour over the remaining half of the sauce or chopped tomatoes chopped tomatoes and scatter over the remaining diced mozzarella. Cook in a preheated oven, 200°C (400°F), Gas Mark 6, for 15–20 minutes until bubbling and golden. Serve hot with a dollop of soured cream, if desired.

Leek and Mushroom Pasty

Serves 4

50 g (2 oz) butter
2 leeks, trimmed and sliced
500 g (1 lb) mushrooms, halved
  (or quartered, if very large)
200 g (7 oz) cream cheese
1 teaspoon dried tarragon or
  1 tablespoon chopped tarragon
500 g (1 lb) puff pastry
flour, for dusting
1 small egg, lightly beaten
salt and pepper

- Melt the butter in a large frying pan and cook the leeks over a medium heat for 3 minutes, stirring occasionally, until they begin to soften. Add the mushrooms and continue to cook for a further 4–5 minutes until tender and lightly golden, then stir in the cream cheese and tarragon.

- Meanwhile, roll out the pastry on a lightly floured surface and cut into 4 x 20 cm (8 inch) circles. Brush a 1 cm (½ inch) border with a little beaten egg.

- Season the leek and mushrooms with a pinch each of salt and pepper and divide the mixture between the 4 circles. Now bring up 2 sides of the pastry to encase the filling, crimping the pastry together with your fingers to seal the edges.

- Arrange the filled pastries on a baking sheet, brush with the remaining beaten egg and cook in a preheated oven, 200°C (400°F), Gas Mark 6, for about 18 minutes until puffed up and golden. Serve warm.

 Buttery Leek and Mushrooms on Toast Melt 75 g (3 oz) butter in a frying pan and add 2 sliced leeks and 250 g (8 oz) sliced mushrooms with 1 teaspoon dried tarragon or 1 tablespoon fresh tarragon, if desired, and a pinch of salt and pepper. Cook over a medium heat for 8–10 minutes, stirring occasionally, until soft and golden. Meanwhile, toast 4 thick slices of bread, spread each with 1 tablespoon cream cheese and arrange on plates. Spoon the buttery leeks and mushrooms over the toast to serve.

Leek and Mushroom Frittata Melt 50 g (2 oz) butter in a large frying pan and cook the leeks and mushrooms as above. Add 565 g (1 lb 2½ oz) canned potatoes, drained and sliced, to the pan for the final minute, to heat. Meanwhile, beat 5 eggs with a pinch each of salt and pepper and 1 teaspoon dried tarragon (optional). Pour the eggs into the pan, stir to combine and cook over a medium-low heat for 5–6 minutes until almost set. Sprinkle over 3 tablespoons finely grated Parmesan cheese or other hard Italian cheese and cook under a grill preheated to a medium setting for 3–4 minutes until the frittata is set. Serve in wedges, with salad.

Skint Smoked Salmon and Cream Cheese Bagel

Serves 4

4 plain or onion bagels, split
6 tablespoons plain or chive
and onion cream cheese
¼ cucumber, sliced (optional)
125 g (4 oz) smoked salmon
trimmings
1 tablespoon chopped chives
(optional)
4 teaspoons lemon juice
pepper

- Arrange the bagels, cut side up, on a baking sheet and toast under a grill preheated to a medium setting for 2–3 minutes until golden.

- Spread the bottom halves if the bagels with the cream cheese and top with the cucumber, if using. Scatter the smoked salmon trimmings over the cucumber and sprinkle over the chopped chives, if using. Drizzle with lemon juice and season generously with pepper.

- Top with the lid and serve.

 Skint Smoked Salmon Scramble
Melt 50 g (2 oz) butter in a large non-stick saucepan and gently cook 2 finely chopped shallots for 7–8 minutes until really soft. Beat 8 eggs in a bowl with 75 ml (3 fl oz) milk, 50 g (2 oz) cream cheese and a generous pinch of black pepper. Pour the mixture into the saucepan and stir gently over a very low heat for 5–6 minutes until the eggs are lightly set but still creamy. Meanwhile, toast 4 bagels as above, or 8 small slices of granary bread. Spread with butter and arrange on serving plates. Spoon the scrambled egg onto the bagels or toast and scatter over 125 g (4 oz) smoked salmon trimmings. Garnish with 1 tablespoon chopped chives, if desired, and season with black pepper.

Skint Smoked Salmon and Herb Tart Unroll a 320 g (11 oz) puff pastry sheet and use it to line a 23 cm (9 inch) tart tin. Scatter 125 g (4 oz) smoked salmon trimmings over the base. In a bowl, lightly beat 4 eggs, 2 tablespoons cream cheese, 1 tablespoon chopped chives, a pinch of salt and a generous pinch of pepper. Pour the mixture over the salmon and cook in a preheated oven, 200°C (400°F), Gas Mark 6, for 20–25 minutes until golden. Slice into wedges and serve hot or cold.

2 🕐 Creamy Chicken and Mushroom Soup

Serves 4

2 tablespoons olive or
  vegetable oil

1 onion, chopped

1 celery stick or leek, chopped

400 g (13 oz) mushrooms,
  chopped

750 ml (1¼ pints) hot chicken
  or vegetable stock

225 g (7½ oz) cooked chicken,
  shredded

50 ml (2 fl oz) single or double
  cream

salt and pepper

crusty bread, to serve (optional)

- Heat the oil in a large saucepan and cook the onion and celery or leek over a medium heat for 7–8 minutes until softened. Stir in the mushrooms and cook for a further 3–4 minutes until softened, then pour in the hot stock, bring to the boil, then simmer gently for 5–6 minutes until all the vegetables are tender.

- Remove from the heat and use a hand-held blender to blend until almost smooth. (Alternatively, if you don't have a blender, push the soup through sieve, or serve as chunky soup.) Stir in the shredded chicken and cream, then season to taste and stir over the heat for 1 final minute until hot but not boiling. Ladle into mugs and serve with crusty bread, if desired.

---

1 🕐 Creamy Grilled Mushrooms

Brush 12 large flat mushrooms with oil and arrange on a foil-lined baking sheet. Sprinkle with salt and pepper and cook under a grill preheated to a medium setting for 4–5 minutes until tender. Remove from the grill, top each one with a tablespoon of a full-fat soft cheese with garlic and herbs (such as Boursin) and return to the grill for a further 1–2 minutes until the cheese is melting. Serve on toasted bread or with mixed salad leaves.

3 Creamy Chicken and Mushroom Pie

Melt a knob of butter in a frying pan and cook 2 trimmed and sliced leeks and 400 g (13 oz) halved mushrooms for 7–8 minutes, stirring occasionally, until softened, then tip into a bowl with 150 g (5 oz) ready-made cheese, carbonara or béchamel sauce, 225 g (7½ oz) cooked shredded chicken and 75 g (3 oz) full-fat soft cheese with garlic and herbs (such as Boursin). Mix to combine, then spoon into a medium-sized ovenproof dish. Spoon 500 g

(1 lb) cold mashed potato on top of the filled pie dish and sprinkle over 100 g (3½ oz) grated Cheddar cheese (or similar). Bake in a preheated oven, 200°C (400°F), Gas Mark 6, for 15–18 minutes, until crisp and golden.

Chilli Corn Fritters

Serves 4

50 g (2 oz) self-raising flour
2 eggs
2 tablespoons sweet chilli sauce,
 plus extra for dipping
2 x 198 g (7 oz) cans sweetcorn,
 drained
50 g (2 oz) butter
salt and pepper

- Place the flour in a bowl and add the eggs and sweet chilli sauce. Whisk to combine, then gently stir the sweetcorn and seasoning into the mixture.

- Melt about a third of the butter in a frying pan and drop 5–6 tablespoons of the mixture into the pan in separate puddles, flattening each one gently. Cook gently over a medium-low heat for about 3 minutes until the bases of the fritters are golden, then flip over each one carefully and cook the other side for 2–3 minutes.

- Repeat with the remaining butter and sweetcorn mixture until you have used up all the batter and made about 16 fritters.

- Serve hot with extra chilli sauce for dipping, if desired.

Chilli Corn Cheese Muffins

Split 4 wholemeal English muffins in half and toast in a toaster until lightly golden. Meanwhile, place 150 g (5 oz) coarsely grated Double Gloucester or Cheddar cheese in a bowl with 3 tablespoons sweet chilli sauce, 2 tablespoons chopped chives (optional) and the drained sweetcorn from a 198 g (7 oz) can. Season with salt and pepper and mix to combine. Spread thickly over the muffins, arrange on a lined baking sheet and cook under a grill preheated to a medium setting for 3–4 minutes until golden and melted. Serve hot with extra sweet chilli sauce.

Chilli Corn Muffins

Sift 225 g (7½ oz) plain flour into a bowl with 1 teaspoon baking powder and ½ teaspoon each of salt and pepper. Rub 50 g (2 oz) butter into the flour until the mixture resembles breadcrumbs, then stir in 1 tablespoon chopped chives (optional). Set aside. In a jug, whisk 1 egg with 2 tablespoons sweet chilli sauce, 125 ml (4 fl oz) milk, 75 ml (3 fl oz) vegetable oil and 100 g (3½ oz) drained sweetcorn. Pour the wet ingredients into the dry ingredients and stir until barely combined. Divide the mixture between the greased or paper case-lined cups of a 12-cup muffin tin, sprinkle with 50 g (2 oz) grated Double Gloucester or Cheddar cheese and bake in a preheated oven, 200°C (400°F), Gas Mark 6, for 18–20 minutes until risen and golden.

STU-BREA-XIF

30 Corned Beef Hash

Serves 4

750 g (1½ lb) potatoes, peeled
   and diced
3 tablespoons of oil
1 large onion, chopped
2 garlic cloves, chopped
340 g (11½ oz) can corned beef,
   chopped or crumbled

To serve

4 fried eggs
2 tablespoons chopped parsley
   (optional)
your preferred sauce (such as
   ketchup, barbecue or brown
   sauce) (optional)

- Cook the potatoes in a large pan of boiling water for about 10 minutes until just tender. Drain well.

- Meanwhile, heat 2 tablespoons of the oil in a large non-stick frying pan and cook the onion and garlic over a medium-low heat for 7–8 minutes until softened.

- Add the remaining oil to the pan with the corned beef and drained potatoes and mix well. Continue to cook for about 15 minutes, turning occasionally – but not too often – until crispy and golden.

- Spoon into 4 warmed plates and top with the fried eggs and parsley, if using. Serve immediately with a choice of ketchup, barbecue or brown sauce, if desired.

 Corned Beef and Onion Bagel

Heat 2 tablespoons vegetable oil in a frying pan and add 1 thinly sliced onion. Cook gently for 8–10 minutes until soft and golden. Meanwhile, toast 4 split plain or onion bagels. Mix together 1 tablespoon each of mayonnaise and wholegrain mustard and spread over the bottom half of each toasted bagel. Slice the corned beef from a 340 g (11½ oz) can and arrange over the mustard mayonnaise. Place on serving plates and serve topped with the onions and toasted lid.

 Corned Beef Fritters

In a bowl, whisk 2 eggs with 100 g (3½ oz) self-raising flour, 1 teaspoon baking powder and 100 ml (3½ fl oz) milk until smooth. Add 2 tablespoons chopped parsley (optional), the chopped corned beef from a 340 g (11½ oz) can, 175 g (6 oz) diced cooked potatoes and 2 finely chopped spring onions and mix to combine. Heat 2 tablespoons vegetable oil in a large non-stick frying pan and drop heaped tablespoons of the mixture into the pan, flattening them slightly with the back of the spoon into 10 cm (4 inch) fritters. Cook over a medium heat for about 2 minutes on each side until golden, then drain on kitchen paper and repeat with the remaining mixture, adding extra oil to the pan if necessary, until you have made about 12 fritters. Serve hot with a choice of ketchup, barbecue or brown sauce for dipping.

2 Mustard and Onion Tartlets

Serves 2

215 g (7¼ oz) sheet of pre-rolled
puff pastry
2 tablespoons wholegrain mustard
150 g (5 oz) Brie, sliced
1 tablespoon beaten egg or milk,
to brush
2 spring onions or ½ small red
onion, finely sliced
½ teaspoon dried thyme
(optional)
salad leaves, to serve

- Cut the puff pastry in half to form 2 rectangles and place these on a baking sheet. Spread the mustard over the bases, leaving a 1 cm (½ inch) border, and top with the sliced Brie. Brush the border with the beaten egg or milk.

- Scatter over the spring onion and thyme, if using, and bake in a preheated oven, 200°C (400°F), Gas Mark 6, for 12–15 minutes until crisp and golden.

- Serve with salad leaves.

1 Mustard and Onion Melts

Slice 1 French stick into thick diagonal slices. Spread ½ teaspoon wholegrain mustard over each slice and top with ½ small red onion, very thinly sliced. Top each piece with a slice of goats' cheese and arrange on the rack of a foil-lined grill tray. Cook under a grill preheated to a medium-hot setting for 3–4 minutes or until the cheese is melting. Serve on top of salad leaves with a bottle of French-style vinaigrette.

3 Leek, Mustard and Onion Tart

Melt 50 g (2 oz) butter in a large frying pan, then slice 3 trimmed leeks and 1 red onion and cook in the pan over a medium-low heat, stirring occasionally, for 8–10 minutes until softened. Meanwhile, unroll a 375 g (12 oz) sheet of pre-rolled puff pastry on a baking sheet and lightly score a 1.5 cm (¾ inch) border around the edge. Brush the border with a little beaten egg or milk. Mix together 2 tablespoons wholegrain mustard and 2 tablespoons cream cheese and spread over the base of the pastry, keeping within the border. Top with the softened leek-and-onion mixture, then cover with 150 g (5 oz) sliced Brie. Bake in a preheated oven, 190°C (375°F), Gas Mark 5, for 18–20 minutes until crisp and golden and the cheese has melted.

30 French Onion Soup with Cheesy Croûtons

Serves 2

50 g (2 oz) butter
3 large onions, halved and
  thinly sliced
2 garlic cloves, roughly chopped
1 tablespoon plain flour
500 ml (17 fl oz) hot beef stock
1 teaspoon dried thyme or
  2 teaspoons chopped thyme
1 individual sandwich baguette
100 g (3½ oz) finely grated
  Emmental or Cheddar cheese
salt and pepper

- Melt the butter in a large saucepan and cook the onions over a medium heat for about 15 minutes, stirring occasionally, until soft and golden. Add the garlic and continue for a further 5 minutes until the onion takes on a deeper golden colour. Stir in the flour for 1 minute.

- Stir in the beef stock and thyme, bring to the boil and simmer gently for 8–10 minutes to allow the flavours to develop. Season to taste.

- Meanwhile, slice the baguette and top with the grated cheese. Cook under a grill preheated to a medium-hot setting for 2–3 minutes until the cheese is melting and golden.

- To serve, ladle the soup into 2 deep bowls and top with the cheesy croûtons.

 Cheese and Onion Toasted Sandwich

Thickly slice 150 g (5 oz) Brie or Camembert. Spread each of 2 slices of bread with 1 tablespoon onion chutney and top with the sliced cheese. Scatter over 1 finely sliced spring onion, then top each one with a second slice of bread. Melt 25 g (1 oz) butter in a large frying pan and add the sandwiches to the pan. Toast over a medium-high heat for 1–2 minutes on each side until golden and crispy. Serve hot with salad leaves.

 Cheese and Onion Croque Madame

In a bowl, mix 150 g (5 oz) grated Cheddar cheese or Emmental with ½ red onion, finely sliced, 1 tablespoon wholegrain mustard and 1 tablespoon crème fraîche. Spread this mixture over 2 thick slices of bread, then top each one with 50 g (2 oz) thinly sliced ham. Top with a second slice of bread. Melt 25 g (1 oz) of butter in a large frying pan and lay the sandwiches in the pan. Cook over a medium-low heat for 4–6 minutes, turning once, until golden. Remove from the pan and keep warm while you add 1 tablespoon vegetable oil to the pan and crack 2 eggs into the oil. Cook over a medium heat for 3–5 minutes, depending on how well done you like your eggs, then remove with a fish slice. Arrange the toasted sandwiches on serving plates with green salad and top each one with a fried egg. Serve immediately with a drizzle of vinaigrette over the salad, if desired.

Quick Cauliflower Cheese

Serves 4

1 cauliflower, broken into
  large pieces
50 g (2 oz) plain flour
25 g (1 oz) butter, plus extra
  for greasing
1 teaspoon mustard powder
  (optional)
450 ml (¾ pint) milk
200 g (7 oz) coarsely grated
  cheese (Red Leicester or
  Cheddar cheese work well)
salt and pepper
grilled bacon, sausages or a
  green salad, to serve (optional)

- Bring a large pan of lightly salted water to the boil and cook the cauliflower for 7–8 minutes until just tender. Drain well.

- Meanwhile, place the flour, butter and mustard powder, if using, in a medium-sized saucepan with the milk. Slowly bring to the boil, stirring constantly, until smooth and thickened. Stir in 100 g (3½ oz) of the cheese and, once it has melted, season to taste.

- Tip the cauliflower into a buttered ovenproof dish, pour over the cheesy sauce and sprinkle over the remaining cheese.

- Cook under a grill preheated to a medium-hot setting for 3–4 minutes until golden. (Alternatively, if you do not have a grill, cook in a preheated oven, 200°C/400°F, Gas Mark 6, for 10–12 minutes, until bubbling and golden.)

- Serve with grilled bacon, sausages or plenty of green salad, if desired.

 Creamy Cauliflower Coleslaw

In a large bowl, mix 150 g (5 oz) natural yogurt with 1 teaspoon mild mustard, 3 tablespoons mayonnaise and 2 teaspoons vinegar, then season with a pinch each of salt and pepper. Slice 1 small cauliflower thinly and scrape into the bowl with 2 peeled and coarsely grated carrots. Mix really well to coat in the dressing, then serve with toasted pitta breads.

 Potato and Cauliflower Soup

Melt 25 g (1 oz) butter in a large pan with 1 tablespoon vegetable oil and cook 1 finely chopped onion and 2 large potatoes, peeled and diced, over a medium heat for 8–10 minutes until the onion is softened and lightly golden. Stir in 1 teaspoon cumin seeds and 1 small cauliflower which has been broken into florets, and continue to cook, stirring frequently for 3–4 minutes, until the cauliflower begins to soften slightly. Pour in 900 ml (1½ pints) vegetable stock and bring to the boil. Reduce the heat, cover and simmer gently for about 15 minutes until the vegetables are really tender. Blend with a hand-held blender until smooth or, if you do not own a blender, press through a sieve or colander. Ladle into bowls and serve topped with golden croûtons.

Barbecue Bacon Burger and Cheesy Chips

Serves 2

250 g (8 oz) oven chips
2 tablespoons vegetable oil
4 slices of smoked streaky bacon
300 g (10 oz) minced beef
1 teaspoon dried oregano
½ red onion, very finely chopped
   (optional)
50 g (2 oz) crumbled blue cheese
50 g (2 oz) very finely grated
   Cheddar cheese
salt and pepper

To serve

barbecue sauce
large burger buns, split and
   toasted

- Arrange the chips in a single layer on a large baking sheet and cook in a preheated oven, 220°C (425°F), Gas Mark 7, for 15–18 minutes or according to the packet instructions until crisp and golden.

- Meanwhile, heat the vegetable oil in a medium-sized frying pan and cook the bacon over a medium heat for 4–5 minutes until golden. Remove from the pan and keep warm.

- While the bacon is cooking, mix the minced beef in a bowl with the oregano, onion, blue cheese and a pinch each of salt and pepper. Shape into 2 burgers and cook in the pan a medium heat for 3–5 minutes on each side until cooked through but still juicy.

- Assemble the burgers in burger buns with the frazzled bacon and a dollop of barbecue sauce, adding other fillings of your choice if desired.

- Remove the chips from the oven, tip into bowls and scatter with the grated cheese. Serve alongside the bacon burger.

 Barbecue Bacon Bagel

Arrange 6 slices of thick-cut bacon on the rack of a foil-lined grill tray and brush with 2 tablespoons sticky barbecue marinade. Cook under a grill preheated to a medium setting for 5–7 minutes, turning once, until cooked. Meanwhile, toast 2 plain or sesame bagels and arrange on serving plates. Top each bottom half with 2 tablespoons coleslaw, then lay the bacon slices on top. Finish with a green lettuce leaf and cover with the lid to serve.

 Barbecue Pork Strips

Lay 6 pork belly slices in an ovenproof dish, then pour over 4 tablespoons sticky barbecue marinade and rub it into the meat to coat it really well. Set aside to marinate for at least 15 minutes. Meanwhile, bring a large pan of lightly salted water to the boil. Rinse 150 g (5 oz) easy-cook long-grain rice under running water, then cook in the boiling water for about 15 minutes or according to the packet instructions until just tender, then drain. Arrange the pork belly slices on the rack of a foil-lined grill tray and cook under a preheated medium-hot grill for 4–5 minutes on each side until sticky and cooked through but still juicy. Spoon the rice onto serving plates, top with the barbecue pork strips and drizzle with any juices. Serve immediately with coleslaw, if desired.

2() Tuna and Chive Rice Salad

Serves 4

300 g (10 oz) easy-cook
   long-grain rice
400 g (13 oz) can red kidney
   beans, rinsed and drained
198 g (7 oz) can sweetcorn,
   rinsed and drained
4 spring onions, finely sliced
   (optional)
400 g (13 oz) can tuna, drained
   and flaked
2 tablespoons chopped chives
salt

To serve

little gem or other crunchy
   lettuce leaves
French-style vinaigrette

- Bring a large pan of lightly salted water to the boil, add the rice, then reduce to a simmer and cook the rice for about 15 minutes or according to the packet instructions, until tender. Drain in a sieve and cool under running water. Drain well.

- Meanwhile, place the kidney beans in a large bowl and mix with the sweetcorn, spring onion if using, tuna and chives. Fold through the cold rice and spoon into bowls. Serve with little gem lettuces and French-style vinaigrette.

1() Grilled Tuna and Chive Melts

Cut 2 sandwich baguettes in half horizontally. Mix drained and flaked tuna from a 185 g (6½ oz) can with 1 chopped red pepper, 100 g (3½ oz) drained sweetcorn, 2 sliced spring onions and 1 tablespoon chopped chives. Stir in 4 tablespoons tomato salsa or mayonnaise. Spread thickly over the cut sides of the baguette and top with 150 g (5 oz) grated Cheddar cheese. Arrange on a baking sheet and cook under a grill preheated to a medium setting for 4–5 minutes until melted and golden. Serve with salad.

Tuna, Chive and Potato Gratin

Bring a large pan of lightly salted water to the boil and cook 1 kg (2 lb) large potatoes, peeled and thinly sliced, for about 8 minutes until just tender. Drain through a colander and tip into a large buttered ovenproof dish with 2 tablespoons chopped chives and drained and flaked tuna from a 400 g (13 oz) can. Meanwhile, heat 300 ml (½ pint) milk with 150 ml double cream, 1 finely chopped garlic clove and a generous pinch each of salt and pepper. Bring to boiling point, then remove the mixture from the heat and pour it over the potato and tuna, shaking the dish to combine. Scatter over 125 g (4 oz) grated Emmental or Cheddar cheese and bake in a preheated oven, 220°C (425°F), Gas Mark 7, for 15–20 minutes until bubbling and golden.

Chicken, Cress and Egg Mayonnaise Sandwich Filler

Serves 2

3 eggs
2 tablespoons mayonnaise
½ teaspoon paprika (optional)
125 g (4 oz) cooked chicken
  breast, chopped
salt and pepper

To serve

wholemeal sandwich bread or
  baked potatoes
small handful of salad cress

- Bring a small pan of water to a rolling boil and gently lower the eggs into the water. Cook for 8 minutes to hard boil the eggs. Remove from the water and sit in a bowl under running water until completely cold.

- Meanwhile, place the mayonnaise in a bowl with the paprika, if using, and a pinch each of salt and pepper.

- Once cold, tap the eggs all over to break the shells. Peel away the shell and roughly chop the hardboiled eggs. Mash into the mayonnaise with the chopped chicken and either spread on bread to make sandwiches or spoon onto baked potatoes. Scatter with the cress to serve.

Tandoori Chicken and Cress Sandwich Filler Place 3 tablespoons mayonnaise or natural yogurt in a bowl with 1 tablespoon tandoori paste, 1 teaspoon lemon juice and 1 tablespoon chopped coriander (optional) and stir well to combine. Add 250 g (8 oz) cooked chunky chicken pieces (or use roast chicken with the skin removed, roughly sliced) to the bowl and mix well to coat. Use this mixture to fill tortilla wraps or plain chapattis with a handful of salad cress and a teaspoon of mango chutney.

Chicken, Cress and Onion Sandwich Filler Heat 2 tablespoons vegetable oil in a large frying pan and cook 2 sliced onions for 12–15 minutes until really soft and golden, stirring occasionally. Scrape into a bowl and set aside. Now increase the heat and add an extra tablespoon of oil. Add 200 g (7 oz) thinly sliced chicken breast fillets to the pan and stir-fry for 7–8 minutes, until cooked through. Remove from the pan and allow to rest for 2 minutes. Mix with the onion and use to fill sandwiches or as a topping for baked potato with mustardy or garlic mayonnaise and a handful of salad cress.

STU-BREA-CAW

Bean and Parsley Pâté

Serves 4

2 x 400 g (13 oz) cans beans (such as haricot or cannellini beans), rinsed and drained

3 tablespoons sun-dried tomato paste

2 teaspoons lemon juice

½ teaspoon ground cumin (optional)

4 tablespoons natural or Greek yogurt

2 tablespoons chopped parsley, plus extra to garnish

salt and pepper

hot toast, to serve

- Place the beans in a food processor with the sun-dried tomato paste, lemon juice and ground cumin, if using. Pulse to a thick, rough-textured paste, then add just enough of the yogurt to create a spreadable pâté. (Alternatively, if you do not own a food processor, mash the ingredients together with the back of a fork to serve as a chunky bean pâté.)

- Scrape the pâté into a bowl, stir in the parsley, then season to taste and serve with plenty of hot toast, garnished with extra parsley.

Bean and Parsley Patties

Mix 2 x 400 g (13 oz) cans beans, rinsed and drained, with 2 tablespoons tomato purée, 1 tablespoon mayonnaise, 1 teaspoon ground cumin, 2 tablespoons chopped parsley and a pinch of salt and pepper in a food processor to a rough paste. Use your hands to shape it into 16 patties. Heat 2 tablespoons olive or vegetable oil in a frying pan and cook the patties for 2–3 minutes on each side. Meanwhile, stir 2 teaspoons lemon juice into 150 g (5 oz) natural or Greek yogurt, ½ teaspoon cumin and 2 tablespoons chopped parsley. Season, then serve with the patties and pitta breads.

Bean and Parsley Stew

Heat 2 tablespoons oil in a large saucepan and cook 1 sliced red onion and 1 chopped green pepper over a medium heat for 7–8 minutes. Add 2 sliced garlic cloves and cook for 1–2 minutes until softened. Stir 1 teaspoon each of ground coriander and cumin into the pan and cook for 1 minute, then add a 400 g (13 oz) can plum tomatoes, a 400 g (13 oz) can drained cannellini, borlotti or butter beans, 2 tablespoons sun-dried tomato paste and 300 ml (½ pint) hot vegetable stock. Bring to the boil, then simmer gently for 10–12 minutes until slightly thickened. Add a 300 g (10 oz) can broad beans, rinsed and drained, or 200 g (7 oz) fresh or frozen broad beans and 4 tablespoons roughly chopped parsley. Season to taste and simmer for 4–5 minutes until the beans are tender. Spoon into 4 warmed dishes and serve scattered with extra chopped parsley and lots of crusty bread.

Smoked Salmon and Chive Mayonnaise

Serves 2 as a light lunch or snack or 4 as a small starter

120 g (3¾ oz) smoked salmon trimmings
1 teaspoon lemon juice
3 tablespoons mayonnaise
2 teaspoons chopped chives (optional), plus extra to garnish
salt and pepper

To serve

brown bread, toasted
lemon wedges (optional)

- Place the smoked salmon trimmings in the bowl of a small food processor or mini chopper and add the lemon juice, mayonnaise, chives, if using, and a generous pinch of black pepper. Blend until the salmon is finely chopped but not completely smooth. (Alternatively, if you do not have a food processor, chop the smoked salmon as finely as possible by hand, then place it in a bowl and stir in the other ingredients, mixing well to combine.)

- Scrape the mixture into a small bowl and season with salt to taste. Spread the mixture onto the toast and garnish with chives, if using. Serve with lemon wedges, if desired.

Fresh Salmon and Chive Burgers

Finely chop 250 g (8 oz) boned and skinned salmon fillet in a food processor (or chop the salmon finely by hand). Finely chop 2 spring onions (optional) and add to the salmon with 2 tablespoons mayonnaise or tartare sauce, 1 tablespoon chopped chives and black pepper. Pulse until well combined, then shape into 2 patties. Heat 2 tablespoons oil in a non-stick frying pan and cook over a medium heat for 4–5 minutes on each side until just cooked. Serve on ciabatta rolls with sweet chilli sauce and salad leaves or with rice and lemon wedges.

Canned Salmon and Chive Fishcakes Cut 350 g (11½ oz) peeled and diced potatoes and cook in a pan of lightly salted water for about 10 minutes until tender but firm. Drain well and set aside, uncovered, to cool slightly. Meanwhile, drain and flake the salmon from a 185 g (6½ oz) can into a bowl with the finely grated rind of ½ lemon (optional), 2 tablespoons tartare sauce or mayonnaise and 1 tablespoon finely chopped chives. Season generously with plenty of ground black pepper, then add the potatoes and mash lightly to combine. Form into 4 small fishcakes, coat in 2–3 tablespoons dried breadcrumbs, then chill for about 12 minutes to firm up slightly. Heat 2 tablespoons vegetable or olive oil in a non-stick frying pan and cook the fishcakes over a medium heat for about 5 minutes, turning once, until crisp and golden. Serve with salad leaves and lemon wedges, if desired.

30 Carrot and Feta Potato Cakes

Serves 2

150 g (5 oz) or 1 large carrot, peeled and diced

350 g (11½ oz) potatoes, peeled and diced

1 small egg, lightly beaten

75 g (3 oz) feta cheese

1 teaspoon ground cumin

1 tablespoon chopped parsley (optional)

2 spring onions, chopped

flour, for dusting

3–4 tablespoons vegetable oil

salt and pepper

2 poached or fried eggs, to serve (optional)

- Bring a large pan of lightly salted water to the boil and cook the carrots and potatoes for about 12 minutes until tender. Drain well and mash together until crushed but not completely smooth. Set aside to cool, uncovered, for at least 10 minutes.

- While the potatoes and carrots are cooling, add the beaten egg, feta, cumin, parsley, onion and a pinch each of salt and pepper to the pan and mix well to combine. Use flour-dusted hands to form the mixture into 4 patties.

- Place the oil in a large non-stick frying pan and shallow-fry the patties gently for about 3 minutes on each side until crisp and golden. Drain on kitchen paper and serve with fried or poached eggs, if desired.

---

 1 Feta and Parsley Dip with Carrot Sticks In a bowl, mash 100 g (3½ oz) crumbled feta with 1 tablespoon chopped parsley, 3 tablespoons crème fraîche, 1 teaspoon lemon juice and a generous pinch of ground black pepper. Scrape into an attractive serving dish and serve immediately with sticks of raw carrots and toasted pitta bread, if desired.

 2 Carrot and Feta Bubble and Squeak Place 200 g (7 oz) cooked leftover potatoes and 200 g (7 oz) cooked leftover carrots in a bowl. (Alternatively, use a 300 g/10 oz can potatoes, drained, and 300 g/10 oz can carrots, drained and sliced.) Roughly mash with the egg, cumin, feta, parsley and spring onions, as above. Press into a greased shallow ovenproof dish and cook in a preheated oven, 220°C (425°F), Gas Mark 7, for 12–15 minutes until crisp and golden. Serve hot with a fried or poached egg, if desired.

STU-BREA-QID

10 Thai Grilled Chicken Sandwich

Serves 2

200 g (7 oz) mini chicken fillets
1 tablespoon Thai red or green
  curry paste
2 tablespoons natural yogurt
1 tablespoon mango chutney or
  natural yogurt
1 ciabatta bread, split lengthways
small handful of shredded
  Iceberg lettuce
a quarter of a sliced cucumber

- Place the chicken fillets in a bowl with the curry paste and natural yogurt. Mix together to combine, then arrange on the rack of a foil-lined grill tray and slide under a preheated medium-hot grill. Grill for 7–8 minutes, turning once, until cooked through and lightly charred.

- Meanwhile, spread the mango chutney or natural yogurt inside the ciabatta bread and top with the lettuce and sliced cucumber. Add the cooked chicken fillets, then cut the bread into 4 to serve.

20 Thai Curry Noodle Soup

Heat 1 tablespoon vegetable oil in a medium-sized saucepan or wok and cook 3 chopped spring onions and 2 chopped garlic cloves gently for 2–3 minutes until softened. Stir in 1 tablespoon green or red Thai curry paste for 2 minutes, then pour in 200 ml (7 fl oz) coconut milk and 350 ml (12 fl oz) hot chicken or vegetable stock. Bring to the boil and simmer gently for 7–8 minutes. Add 125 g (4 oz) mangetout or fine green beans and 200 g (7 oz) medium noodles and simmer gently for a further 3–4 minutes or according to packet instructions until the noodles are just tender. Lift out the noodles and heap them into bowls, then pour over the fragrant soup. Garnish with coriander leaves, if desired.

30 Thai Curry Rice Bowl

Heat 2 tablespoons vegetable oil in a frying pan and add 1 roughly chopped onion. Stir-fry for 4–5 minutes until beginning to colour. Cut 250 g (8 oz) skinless chicken thigh fillets into bite-sized pieces and add to the pan for about 10 minutes, stirring frequently, until lightly golden and almost cooked. Stir 1–2 tablespoons (depending on heat required) Thai green curry paste into the pan and stir-fry for 1 minute, stirring constantly to prevent burning. Pour 200 ml (7 fl oz) coconut milk and 125 ml (4 fl oz) hot chicken stock into the pan and simmer gently for about 10 minutes to allow the flavours to develop. Serve spooned over bowls of Thai or long-grain rice, garnished with coriander leaves, if desired.

STU-BREA-VAP

30 Sausage and Cheese Rolls

Serves 4

375 g (12 oz) sheet of pre-rolled puff pastry, about 40 x 25 cm (16 x 10 inch)

3 tablespoons cream cheese or cream cheese with chives, at room temperature

½ small red onion, finely chopped, or 2 finely chopped spring onions

125 g (4 oz) grated Cheddar cheese

8 herby sausages

1 small egg, beaten

- Place the pastry sheet on a clean surface and spread the cream cheese thinly over the surface. Scatter over the chopped onion and 75 g (3 oz) of the grated cheese.

- Cut the pastry lengthways into 2 long strips and arrange 4 sausages, end to end, along the centre of each strip. Roll up the pastry strips to create 2 long sausage-shaped rolls, then cut each roll into 4 individual sausage rolls.

- Arrange the sausage rolls on baking trays lined with kitchen foil, make 2–3 small cuts in the top of each one, then brush with beaten egg and sprinkle over the remaining grated cheese.

- Bake in a preheated oven, 220°C (425°F), Gas Mark 7, for 18–22 minutes or until the sausages are cooked through and the pastry is puffed up and golden. Serve warm or cold as part of a Ploughman's-style lunch or brunch.

10 Grilled Sausage and Cheese Rarebit

Place 4 cut pieces of French bread, cut side up, on a baking sheet and slide under a grill preheated to a medium setting. Grill for 2–3 minutes until lightly toasted. Meanwhile, beat 1 egg in a large bowl and mix well with 150 g (5 oz) grated Cheddar, 2 teaspoons Worcestershire sauce, 1 teaspoon wholegrain mustard and 2 tablespoons milk or beer. Thickly slice 8 Frankfurter-style or leftover cooked sausages and arrange over the toasted baguette. Spoon the cheesy topping over the sausages and return to the grill for 2–3 minutes until the cheese is melted and golden. Serve hot.

20 Sausage and Cheese Fold-Over

Cut a 325 g (11 oz) sheet of pre-rolled puff pastry into quarters and arrange on a baking sheet. Brush each quarter with 1 teaspoon mild mustard and sprinkle with 50 g (2 oz) grated Cheddar cheese. Top each one with 2 Frankfurters, then fold over the pastry and brush with beaten egg. Bake in a preheated oven, 220°C (425°F), Gas Mark 7, for about 15 minutes or until the pastry is puffed up and golden. Serve hot or cold.

STU-BREA-RIW

QuickCook

Brain Food Meals

Recipes listed by cooking time

30

Herby Baked Salmon 76

Marinated Beef with
Broccoli and Brown Rice 78

Citrus Baked Chicken 80

Vegetable Pasta Bake 82

Beef and Potato Balti
with Spinach 84

Green Pepper, Mackerel and
Lentil Curry with Spinach 86

Harissa Lamb Koftas with
Sesame Seeds 88

Red Pepper and
Kidney Bean Soup 90

Sweet Chilli Salmon
Fishcakes 92

Spiced Aubergine
with Chickpeas 94

Healthy Rice, Green Bean
and Broccoli Bowl 96

Sage and Lemon Baked
Turkey Steaks 98

Wholewheat Pasta Bake
with Blue Cheese and
Walnuts 100

Sardine and Brown Rice
Bowl 102

One Pot Tomato and
Chorizo Jambalaya 104

Crunchy Baked Carrots
and Broccoli 106

Fruity Braised
Red Cabbage 108

Tomato, Bacon and
Butter Bean Stew 110

Lime and Ginger
Chicken Bowl 112

Beetroot, Mackerel and
Goats' Cheese Lentils 114

Sardine and Bean Bake 116

Beef and Bean Sprouts
with Peanuts 118

Spaghetti and Meatballs
with Spicy Tomato Sauce 120

Lemony Salmon Goujons 122

20

Herby Pan-Fried Salmon 76

Sizzling Beef and Broccoli
Stir-Fry 78

Citrus Chicken Couscous 80

Vegetable Pasta Bowl 82

Beef Madras Burgers
with Spinach 84

Grilled Mackerel with
Peppers and Couscous 86

Grilled Harissa
Lamb Skewers 88

Red Pepper, Kidney Bean
and Spinach Stew 90

Sweet Chilli Salmon
Quesadillas 92

Spiced Vegetable
and Chickpea Soup 94

Healthy Green Bean
and Broccoli Bowl 96

Sage and Lemon
Stir-Fried Turkey 98

Blue Cheese and
Walnut Wholewheat
Pasta Twists 100

Sardine and Bean
Linguine 102

Spicy Chorizo and Tomato
Pasta 104

10

Carrot and Broccoli
Vegetable Stir-Fry 106

Red Cabbage and
Beetroot Lentils 108

Tomato, Bacon and
Butterbean Soup 110

Lime and Ginger
Chicken Wrap 112

Beetroot and Grilled
Mackerel Salad 114

Warm Sardine, Bean
and Potato Salad 116

Beef Skewers with
Satay Sauce 118

Spicy Tomato
Meatball Wraps 120

Simple Grilled Salmon
with Horseradish Mash 122

Herby Smoked Salmon
Pasta 76

Quick Beef Chow Mein
with Broccoli 78

Citrus Chicken Salad 80

Vegetable Pasta Soup 82

Curried Beef Stir-Fry
with Spinach 84

Flaked Mackerel and
Pepper Couscous 86

Grilled Harissa Lamb Pittas 88

Mixed Pepper, Kidney Bean
and Spinach Salad 90

Smoked Salmon and
Sweet Chilli Baguettes 92

Spiced Chickpea Hummus
with Crudités 94

Healthy Green Bean
and Broccoli Salad 96

Sage, Lemon and Turkey
Ciabatta 98

Blue Cheese and Walnut
Pasta Salad 100

Sardine and Three Bean
Salad 102

Quick Fried Rice with
Tomato and Chorizo 104

Quick Broccoli and
Carrot Couscous 106

Red Cabbage Coleslaw 108

Warm Bacon, Tomato
and Butterbean Salad 110

Lime and Ginger Chicken
Pot Noodle 112

Beetroot Hummus
with Mackerel 114

Sardine and Bean
Couscous 116

Spicy Peanut and Beef
Wrap 118

Spicy Tomato
Meatball Stew 120

Smoked Salmon with
Lemon Mayo 122

 # Herby Pan-Fried Salmon

Serves 4

75 g (3 oz) butter

2 spring onions, finely sliced

3 tablespoons mixed chopped herbs (such as parsley, chives, chervil and tarragon)

1 tablespoon drained capers, rinsed (optional)

1 teaspoon finely grated lemon rind

1 tablespoon lemon juice

4 boneless salmon fillets, about 150 g (5 oz) each, skin on

2 teaspoons olive or vegetable oil

To serve

steamed couscous

lemon wedges

- Melt the butter in a saucepan and cook the spring onions over a medium-low heat for 2–3 minutes until softened. Stir in the chopped herbs, capers, if using, and the lemon rind and juice, then remove from the heat and set aside.

- Meanwhile, rub a little oil over the salmon fillets and heat a frying pan until hot. Cook the salmon, skin side down, over a medium-high heat for 3–4 minutes or until the skin is crispy. Carefully turn over the fillets and cook for a further 3–4 minutes until just cooked but still slightly pink in the middle. Cover with foil and set aside to rest somewhere warm for 2–3 minutes.

- Arrange the salmon fillets in warmed dishes and drizzle over the herby butter. Serve immediately with steamed couscous and lemon wedges.

 ### Herby Smoked Salmon Pasta

Cook 400 g (13 oz) quick-cook pasta (such as spaghetti or penne) in a large pan of lightly salted boiling water for 3–5 minutes or according to the packet instructions until just tender. Drain the pasta and return to the pan, then toss with 4 tablespoons pesto, 120 g (3¾ oz) sliced smoked salmon trimmings, 1 tablespoon lemon juice and 3 tablespoons crème fraîche. Season with black pepper and heap into warmed bowls to serve.

 ### Herby Baked Salmon

Place 75 g (3 oz) softened butter in a bowl and mix with 3 tablespoons mixed chopped herbs, 1 teaspoon finely grated lemon rind and a pinch each of salt and pepper. Smear the herby butter over 4 chunky boneless salmon fillets and arrange in a foil-lined ovenproof dish. Cover with foil, scrunching the edges together to seal, then bake in a preheated oven, 180°C (350°F), Gas Mark 4, for 18–20 minutes until the salmon is just cooked, but still slightly pink in the middle. Remove from the oven and set aside to rest for 2–3 minutes, then scatter over 1 tablespoon drained capers and 2 sliced spring onions and serve with steamed couscous or new potatoes, with lemon wedges and rocket leaves, if desired.

STU-BRAI-KAT

Sizzling Beef and Broccoli Stir-Fry

Serves 2

1 tablespoon vegetable or sesame oil

150 g (5 oz) trimmed rump steak, cut into thin strips

1 onion, sliced

1 red pepper, cut into strips

150 g (5 oz) broccoli, broken into small florets

small handful of bean sprouts (optional)

175 g (6 oz) dried fine egg noodles

120 g (3¾ oz) black bean stir-fry sauce, or similar

- Heat the oil in a frying pan or wok and cook the steak over a medium-high heat for about 2 minutes, stirring occasionally, until browned, then remove with a slotted spoon and set aside.

- Return the pan to the heat, adding a little extra oil if necessary, and stir-fry the onion and peppers for 2–3 minutes until they begin to soften. Stir the broccoli into the pan and cook for a further 2 minutes, then add the bean sprouts, if using, and cook for 1–2 minutes, just until they begin to wilt.

- Meanwhile, cook the noodles for about 3 minutes or according to the packet instructions until just tender.

- Return the beef to the pan to reheat, add the black bean sauce, then tip the drained noodles into the pan and toss quickly to combine. Heap into 2 warmed bowls to serve.

 Quick Beef Chow Mein with Broccoli

Heat 2 tablespoons vegetable oil in a frying pan and cook the beef as above, then remove with a slotted spoon and set aside. Add 200 g (7 oz) broccoli florets to the pan with 2 sliced spring onions and stir-fry for 2–3 minutes until almost tender. Tip 250 g (8 oz) fresh cooked noodles into the pan and stir-fry for a further 2–3 minutes until tender and hot. Return the beef to the pan with a 120 g (3¾ oz) packet of chow mein stir-fry sauce and stir to heat. Heap into bowls and serve immediately.

Marinated Beef with Broccoli and Brown Rice Place 1 thick rump steak, about 200 g (7 oz) in weight, into a dish and pour over 2 tablespoons sweet teriyaki marinade, 2 teaspoons peeled and grated fresh root ginger and 1 crushed garlic clove. Rub the marinade all over the steak and set aside in the refrigerator for at least 10 minutes. Heat 1 tablespoon vegetable oil a frying pan and cook the steak over a medium-high heat for 3–4 minutes on each side until browned but still pink. Remove from the pan and set aside somewhere warm to rest. Clean the pan and return to a medium heat with 1 tablespoon oil. Stir-fry 150 g (5 oz) broccoli florets for 3–4 minutes until just tender, then remove the broccoli from the pan. Slice the beef thickly, then toss with the broccoli and arrange over 2 bowls of cooked brown rice. Pour 4 tablespoons sweet teriyaki marinade into the pan to heat, then remove from the heat and drizzle the heated marinade over the beef and broccoli to serve.

STU-BRAI-WYY

1 Citrus Chicken Salad

Serves 2

1 orange
4 cooked roast chicken thighs
75 g (3 oz) watercress
1 avocado, stoned, peeled
  and sliced
2 teaspoons walnut or olive oil
shelled walnut pieces (optional)

- Place the orange on a chopping board and use a small sharp knife to cut off the top and bottom so that you cut right through the peel and outside pith to the flesh. Now cut the remaining peel and pith away from the flesh, cutting in strips downwards, following the curve of the orange. Cut the orange into fleshy segments, using a sharp knife to carefully cut either side of the inside pith. Discard the peel and pith, keeping only the segments.

- Slice or shred the cooked chicken thighs, discarding the bones and skin, if preferred. Divide the watercress between 2 plates and arrange the orange segments, chicken and sliced avocado attractively over the watercress. Drizzle with walnut oil and scatter over a few walnut pieces, if desired.

2 Citrus Chicken Couscous

Place 2 chicken breasts between 2 pieces of clingfilm and batter with a rolling pin or the base of a saucepan to flatten. Place in a dish with 2 teaspoons finely grated lemon rind, 2 tablespoons olive oil, 1 teaspoon chopped thyme leaves (optional), 1 crushed garlic clove and a generous pinch of black pepper. Rub the chicken well with all the flavours. Heat a large dry frying pan and cook the chicken over a medium heat for 3–4 minutes each side or until golden and the juices run clear when the flesh is pierced with a skewer. Remove from the heat, cover and rest for 2–3 minutes. Meanwhile, place

125 g (4 oz) couscous in a bowl with a small knob of butter and 1 tablespoon lemon juice, then pour over 125 ml (4 fl oz) boiling chicken stock. Cover and set aside for 5–8 minutes or until the grains are tender and the liquid has been absorbed. Fluff up the couscous with a fork, then spoon into 2 warmed dishes and top with the chicken and its juices to serve.

3 Citrus Baked Chicken

Wrap 4 rindless streaky bacon rashers around 2 chicken breasts and pan-fry in 1 tablespoon olive oil over a medium–high heat for 2 minutes on each side until golden. Meanwhile, warm 200 ml (7 fl oz) orange juice in a pan with ½ teaspoon dried thyme and 2 teaspoons wholegrain mustard. Put the chicken in an ovenproof dish, pour over the juice and bake in a preheated oven, 200°C (400°F), Gas Mark 6, for about 20 minutes until the chicken is cooked through. Slice thickly, arrange on 2 warmed plates, drizzle over the orangey juices and serve with a watercress and avocado salad.

Vegetable Pasta Bowl

Serves 4

4 tablespoons olive or
  vegetable oil
2 garlic cloves, sliced
400 g (13 oz) pasta shells or bows
400 g (13 oz) broccoli florets
200 g (7 oz) green beans, halved
12 cherry tomatoes, halved
2–3 tablespoons lemon juice
salt and pepper

- Warm the oil in a small pan and add the sliced garlic. Heat the pan gently for 1–2 minutes to soften the garlic and flavour the oil. Remove from the heat and set aside to infuse.

- Bring a pan of lightly salted water to the boil and cook the pasta for 10–12 minutes or according to the packet instructions. Add the broccoli and green beans for the final 3–4 minutes of cooking time. When the vegetables and pasta are just tender, drain well, reserving 2 tablespoons of the cooking liquid.

- Stir the cherry tomatoes gently into the pasta and vegetables with the warm garlicky oil, reserved water and the lemon juice, to taste. Season with a pinch of salt and plenty of black pepper, then spoon into 4 bowls to serve.

 Vegetable Pasta Soup

Heat 2 tablespoons oil in a pan and cook 2 sliced garlic cloves gently for 1 minute. Pour in 900 ml (1½ pints) hot vegetable stock, bring to the boil, add 150 g (5 oz) vermicelli or other very small pasta shape and simmer for 2–3 minutes. Add 300 g (10 oz) broccoli florets and 2 coarsely grated courgettes. Return to the boil and simmer for 3–5 minutes until the vegetables and pasta are tender. Serve immediately with plenty of crusty bread.

 Vegetable Pasta Bake

Cook 300 g (10 oz) penne in a large pan of lightly salted boiling water for 11 minutes or according to the packet instructions until just tender. Drain and return to the pan. Meanwhile, heat 2 tablespoons olive or vegetable oil in a large frying pan and cook 1 chopped onion and 1 chopped red pepper for 6–7 minutes over a medium-high heat until softened. Add 1 coarsely grated courgette, 125 g (4 oz) sliced mushrooms and 150 g (5 oz) small broccoli florets (optional) and cook for a further 2–3 minutes until the vegetables begin to soften. Stir in 400 g (13 oz) tomato-based pasta sauce or chopped tomatoes and simmer gently for 2–3 minutes until the vegetables are almost tender. Pour the sauce over the drained pasta with 150 g (5 oz) crème fraîche (optional, for a creamier bake), then season and tip into a large ovenproof dish. Top with 125 g (4 oz) grated cheese and bake in a preheated oven, 220°C (425°F), Gas Mark 7, for 12–15 minutes, until bubbling and golden.

30 Beef and Potato Balti with Spinach

Serves 4

3 tablespoons vegetable oil
450 g (14½ oz) stir-fry beef strips
1 red pepper, cut into large
  chunks
1 onion, thickly sliced
250 g (8 oz) sweet potato,
  peeled and diced
500 g (1 lb) balti cooking sauce
3 tomatoes, cut into wedges
200 g (7 oz) spinach, washed and
  roughly chopped

- Heat 2 tablespoons of the oil in a pan set over a medium-high heat and cook the beef for 3–4 minutes, stirring occasionally, until browned and just cooked through. Remove from the pan with a slotted spoon and set aside. Return the pan to the heat.

- Add the remaining oil to the pan and cook the pepper, onion and sweet potato for 5–6 minutes, stirring frequently, until lightly coloured and softened.

- Stir the balti sauce into the pan with the tomato wedges, then reduce the heat, cover and simmer gently for about 15 minutes or until the vegetables are tender and the sauce has thickened slightly.

- Return the beef to the pan, add the spinach and stir over the heat for 1–2 minutes until the beef is hot and the spinach has wilted. Serve immediately.

 1 Curried Beef Stir-Fry with Spinach Heat 2 tablespoons oil in a frying pan and cook 450 g (14½ oz) beef stir-fry strips over a high heat for 2 minutes until browned all over. Add 1 thinly sliced onion and cook for 2 minutes. Reduce the heat, stir in 2 tablespoons Madras or balti curry paste and cook for 1 minute. Pour in 400 ml (14 fl oz) reduced-fat coconut milk and 200 ml (7 fl oz) hot beef or vegetable stock. Simmer gently for 2 minutes. Stir in 200 g (7 oz) roughly chopped spinach until just wilted. Serve with naan bread or rice.

 2 Beef Madras Burgers with Spinach In a bowl, combine 400 g (13 oz) minced beef with 1 small very finely chopped onion, 1 tablespoon Madras curry paste and 2 tablespoons chopped coriander or parsley. Mix really well with your hands, then shape into 4 patties. Heat 2 tablespoons vegetable oil in a frying pan and cook the burgers over a medium heat for 4–5 minutes on each side until cooked through but still juicy. Meanwhile, if desired, mix 1 teaspoon lemon juice, ½ teaspoon ground cumin and a pinch each of salt and pepper into 4 tablespoons natural yogurt. Arrange the cooked burgers in burger buns, naan breads or pitta breads and top each one with a small handful of young spinach leaves. Serve with sliced cucumber and a dollop of the spiced yogurt or some mango chutney.

10 Flaked Mackerel and Pepper Couscous

Serves 4

250 g (8 oz) couscous
300 ml (½ pint) hot vegetable
 stock or water
1 green pepper, diced
2 spring onions, finely sliced
small bunch of parsley, chopped
2 smoked mackerel fillets, skinned
 and flaked

For the dressing

1 tablespoon harissa or sundried
 tomato paste
4 tablespoons olive or
 vegetable oil
1½ tablespoons lemon juice

- Place the couscous in a bowl and pour over the boiling stock. Cover and set aside for 5–6 minutes until just tender.

- Combine the dressing ingredients in a small bowl or jug.

- Fork the pepper, onions and parsley through the couscous with 2 tablespoons of the dressing. Spoon the couscous salad onto plates and scatter over the flaked mackerel. Serve with the dressing on the side, for drizzling on top.

 20 Grilled Mackerel with Peppers and Couscous Mix together 4 tablespoons vegetable oil, 2 teaspoons grated lemon rind, 3 crushed garlic cloves and 1 tablespoon grated fresh root ginger. Place 8 small boned mackerel fillets and 2 red peppers, cut into wedges, in a shallow dish. Pour over the marinade, mixing to coat. Set aside for 5–10 minutes. Arrange the mackerel fillets and peppers on the rack of a foil-lined grill tray, skin side up, then cook under a grill preheated to its highest setting for 4–5 minutes, turning once. Serve with steamed couscous, drizzled with any juices.

 30 Green Pepper, Mackerel and Lentil Curry with Spinach Cut 400 g (13 oz) boned mackerel fillets into large chunks and place in a bowl with 3 tablespoons curry paste (such as tikka masala paste). Mix thoroughly to coat the mackerel in the spices, then set aside. Now heat 2 tablespoons vegetable oil in a large frying pan and cook 1 chopped green pepper over a medium heat for 6–7 minutes. Add 2 chopped garlic cloves and 1 tablespoon peeled and chopped fresh root ginger (optional) and cook for a further 2 minutes until softened. Scrape the mackerel into the pan and stir over the heat for 2 minutes to cook the spices. Pour 200 ml (7 fl oz) coconut milk, 300 ml (½ pint) hot vegetable stock and the rinsed and drained lentils from a 400 g (13 oz) can into the pan, bring to the boil, then reduce the heat and simmer gently for about 12 minutes until the fish is cooked and the curry has thickened. Stir in 200 g (7 oz) thawed frozen leaf spinach and cook for a further 1–2 minutes until hot, then serve spooned over cooked couscous or rice or with plenty of warmed naan bread.

STU-BRAI-ZUT

10 Grilled Harissa Lamb Pittas

Serves 2

2 lamb steaks, about 150 g
(5 oz) each
1 teaspoon finely grated
lemon rind
1 tablespoon olive oil
2–4 teaspoons harissa
4 tablespoons hummus
2 wholemeal pitta breads

To serve (optional)

lemon wedges
rocket leaves

- Place the lamb steaks in a dish with the lemon rind, oil and 1–2 teaspoons harissa and rub to coat. Arrange the coated steaks on the rack of a foil-lined grill tray and cook under a grill preheated to a medium-high setting for 5–7 minutes, turning once, until cooked but still slightly pink in the middle. Remove and set aside to rest for 1–2 minutes.

- Meanwhile, stir 1–2 teaspoons harissa into the hummus. Lightly toast the pittas in a toaster, then arrange on warmed plates and top with a dollop of hummus. Arrange the lamb steaks on top of the hummus, drizzled with any juices. Serve with lemon wedges and rocket leaves, if desired.

---

 20 Grilled Harissa Lamb Skewers

Mix 1 tablespoon harissa with 2 tablespoons natural yogurt, 1 teaspoon finely grated lemon rind, 1 tablespoon chopped mint (optional) and ½ teaspoon cumin seeds. Mix with 250 g (4 oz) cubed lamb and mix well to coat. Set aside for at least 5 minutes. Thread onto skewers, arrange on the rack of a foil-lined grill tray and cook under a grill preheated to a medium-high setting for 6–8 minutes until charred but still slightly pink. Rest for 1–2 minutes, then serve the skewers with couscous and hummus.

 30 Harissa Lamb Koftas with Sesame Seeds Place 250 g (8 oz) minced lamb in a bowl with ½ teaspoon ground cumin, 1 teaspoon finely grated lemon rind and 2 teaspoons harissa and mix thoroughly with your hands to form 8–10 slightly flattened meatball shapes. Chill in the refrigerator for 10 minutes. Meanwhile, boil 150 g (5 oz) rinsed long-grain rice in a pan of lightly salted water for about 15 minutes or according to the packet instructions until just tender. Heat 2 tablespoons oil in a frying pan and cook the koftas gently for 8–10 minutes until cooked and golden. Take the pan off the heat and sprinkle over 2 teaspoons sesame seeds, shaking the pan to coat. Drain the rice and spoon onto 2 warmed plates. Top with the koftas, then sprinkle over 1 tablespoon chopped parsley (optional) and 1 teaspoon sesame seeds. Serve immediately with a generous dollop of harissa hummus, made as above.

STU-BRAI-WUU

Red Pepper, Kidney Bean and Spinach Stew

Serves 4

3 tablespoons olive or
    vegetable oil
2 large red peppers, cut into
    large pieces
3 garlic cloves, sliced
2 teaspoons ground cumin or
    Mexican spice mix, such as
    fajita seasoning (optional)
2 tablespoons tomato purée
400 ml (14 fl oz) hot vegetable
    stock
400 g (13 oz) can chopped
    tomatoes
610 g (1 lb 3¾ oz) canned kidney
    beans, rinsed and drained
200 g (7 oz) frozen leaf spinach,
    defrosted and drained
salt and pepper

- Heat the oil in a saucepan and cook the peppers and garlic over a medium heat for 5–6 minutes, stirring frequently, until softened.

- Stir in the cumin, if using, and cook for 1 minute before adding the tomato purée, hot stock, chopped tomatoes and kidney beans. Bring to the boil, season to taste, then cover and simmer gently for 10–12 minutes until thickened slightly. Stir in the spinach for the final minute of cooking, then ladle into bowls to serve.

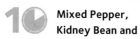 **Mixed Pepper, Kidney Bean and Spinach Salad** In a bowl, mix 1 red and 1 green pepper, finely chopped, ½ cucumber, diced, and 1 small bunch of chopped coriander or parsley with a 400g (13 oz) can kidney beans, rinsed and drained. Drizzle over 3 tablespoons each of oil and lime juice, then season to taste and toss gently with 150 g (5 oz) young spinach leaves to serve.

Red Pepper and Kidney Bean Soup Cook the peppers and garlic as above until softened. Add the ground cumin and cook for a minute, then pour in 750 ml (1¼ pints) hot vegetable stock, 500 g (1 lb) sieved tomatoes or passata and 2 x 400 g (13 oz) cans kidney beans, rinsed and drained, reserving about 200 g (7 oz) of the beans. Season with a pinch each of salt and pepper, then cover, bring to a boil and simmer for about 15 minutes until slightly thickened. Use a hand-held blender to blend the soup (alternatively, if you don't have a blender, serve it as a chunky bean soup), then stir through the reserved beans and 150 g (5 oz) defrosted chopped spinach and heat through. Ladle into bowls to serve, scattered with chopped parsley, if desired.

30 Sweet Chilli Salmon Fishcakes

Serves 2

250 g (8 oz) chunky boneless
and skinless salmon fillet,
roughly diced

1 tablespoon sweet chilli sauce

1 small garlic clove, crushed
(optional)

2 spring onions, finely chopped

2 tablespoons finely chopped
coriander

1 teaspoon finely grated lime
rind (optional)

2 tablespoons vegetable oil

- Place the diced salmon in a food processor with the chilli
sauce, garlic, spring onions, coriander and lime rind and pulse
quickly until chopped together, but not smooth. (Alternatively,
if you do not own a food processor, chop the salmon as finely
as possible before mixing with the remaining ingredients.)
Scrape into a bowl, then use damp hands to shape into
2 patties. Arrange on a plate, cover with clingfilm and chill
in the refrigerator for 10–12 minutes to firm up slightly.

- Heat the oil in a large non-stick frying pan and cook the
fishcakes over a medium heat for 5–6 minutes each side
until golden and cooked through. Serve immediately with
steamed or egg fried rice.

 **Smoked Salmon
and Sweet Chilli
Baguettes** In a small bowl,
mix 1 tablespoon sweet chilli
sauce with 2 tablespoons cream
cheese and 1 tablespoon chopped
coriander (optional). Spread
over 2 split individual sandwich
baguettes and scatter over
1 small ripe but firm avocado,
diced, and 1 finely sliced spring
onion. Top each baguette with
about 50 g (2 oz) sliced smoked
salmon trimmings, then squeeze
over a little lime juice (optional).
Season with black pepper,
garnish with a few rocket leaves,
then serve with extra sweet
chilli sauce, if desired.

 **Sweet Chilli
Salmon Quesadillas**
Rub a little oil over 1 chunky
salmon fillet that weighs about
200 g (7 oz) and season with
a little salt and pepper. Heat
a non-stick frying pan and
cook the salmon fillet for about
4 minutes on each side until
just cooked through. Cover
with foil and set aside to rest
for 2–3 minutes. Arrange 2 large
soft tortilla wraps on a clean
surface and scatter with 2 thinly
sliced spring onions and 1 ripe
but firm avocado, diced. Flake
the salmon over the avocado
and drizzle each tortilla with
2 teaspoons sweet chilli sauce,

then top each one with a
second tortilla. Toast the
quesadillas, one at a time, in a
large dry frying pan for about
4 minutes, carefully turning over
mid-way through cooking, until
toasted and golden. Cut into
slices and serve hot with lime
wedges, if desired.

Spiced Vegetable and Chickpea Soup

Serves 4

2 tablespoons olive or
vegetable oil

1 onion, chopped

1 green or red pepper, chopped

1 aubergine, diced

2 teaspoons peeled and chopped
fresh root ginger

1 teaspoon chilli flakes

6 tomatoes, roughly diced

900 ml (1½ pints) hot vegetable
stock

400 g (13 oz) can chickpeas,
rinsed and drained

salt and pepper

- Heat the oil in a large saucepan and cook the vegetables and ginger for 7–8 minutes until slightly softened. Add the chilli flakes, tomatoes, hot stock and chickpeas and bring to the boil. Reduce the heat and simmer gently for about 10 minutes until the vegetables are tender.

- Use a hand-held blender to blend until smooth. (Alternatively, if you don't have a blender, serve it as a chunky soup.) Season to taste, then ladle into mugs to serve.

 Spiced Chickpea Hummus with Crudités Heat 2 tablespoons olive or vegetable oil in a small frying pan and cook 2 chopped garlic cloves and 1 teaspoon chilli flakes over a low heat for 2–3 minutes until softened. Scrape into a food processor with 1 teaspoon ground cumin, 1 tablespoon lemon juice and 2 tablespoons natural yogurt. Process until smooth, then season to taste, scrape into a bowl and serve with lots of raw vegetable dippers (such as carrot, cucumber and celery sticks, broccoli and cauliflower florets, cherry tomatoes, button mushrooms, radishes and mixed pepper strips).

 Spiced Aubergine with Chickpeas Cut 2 aubergines into bite-sized pieces, then mix in a bowl with 1 chopped onion, 1 chopped green pepper and 1 tablespoon harissa. Heat 3 tablespoons olive or vegetable oil in a large saucepan and cook the vegetables over a medium heat for about 6–7 minutes, stirring frequently, until slightly softened. Stir in 2 x 400 g (13 oz) cans chopped tomatoes and a 400 g (13 oz) can chickpeas, rinsed and drained. Season to taste, then cover and simmer gently for about 15 minutes until the vegetables are tender. Serve the spiced aubergine with couscous, if desired.

10 Healthy Green Bean and Broccoli Salad

Serves 2

200 g (7 oz) mixture of broccoli florets and fine green beans
400 g (13 oz) canned borlotti or aduki beans, rinsed and drained
1 celery stick, finely chopped
½ small red onion, finely sliced
1 small ripe avocado, stoned, peeled and diced
1 tablespoon sunflower seeds

For the dressing

1 tablespoon lime or lemon juice
2 tablespoons groundnut or vegetable oil
1 tablespoon light soy sauce

- Cook the green beans and broccoli in a pan of lightly salted boiling water for 2–3 minutes until lightly cooked. Drain and cool under cold water.

- Meanwhile, combine the canned beans in a bowl with the celery, onion and avocado.

- Whisk together the dressing ingredients in a small bowl.

- Add the cold beans to the salad and gently fold through the dressing. Spoon into a serving dish and scatter with the sunflower seeds.

20 Healthy Green Bean and Broccoli Bowl

Heat 2 tablespoons groundnut or vegetable oil in a frying pan or wok and cook 1 sliced onion and 1 sliced red pepper over a high heat for 3–4 minutes until they begin to soften. Add 1 chopped garlic clove and 1 teaspoon peeled and chopped fresh root ginger for a further minute. Stir 150 g (5 oz) halved green beans into the pan with 150 g (5 oz) broccoli florets and stir-fry for 3–4 minutes until the vegetables are almost tender. Now stir 150 g (5 oz) bean sprouts into the pan and cook for a further 2–3 minutes until the vegetables are just tender. Remove from the heat, toss with 1 tablespoon light soy sauce and heap into bowls to serve, scattered with a teaspoon of sesame seeds and extra soy sauce, if desired.

30 Healthy Rice, Green Bean and Broccoli Bowl

Cook 175 g (6 oz) brown rice in a pan of salted boiling water for 20–25 minutes until tender. Cool under cold water and drain. Meanwhile, cook 125 g (4 oz) fine green beans and 150 g (5 oz) broccoli florets in a pan of salted boiling water for 2–3 minutes until almost tender. Cool under cold water and drain. Combine a 210 g (7¹/₃ oz) can kidney beans, drained and rinsed, with a 198 g (7 oz) can sweetcorn, drained, and 1 sliced spring onion. Add the rice with the broccoli, 2 tablespoons chopped coriander, and 1 tablespoon lime or lemon juice. Stir to combine, then spoon into dishes to serve.

Sage and Lemon Stir-Fried Turkey

Serves 2

2 tablespoons olive or vegetable oil

250 g (8 oz) stir-fry turkey strips

finely grated rind and juice of ½ lemon

1 garlic clove, crushed

2 teaspoons shredded sage leaves, plus extra to garnish

325 ml (11 fl oz) hot vegetable stock

150 g (5 oz) bulgar wheat

steamed green beans or mangetout, to serve (optional)

- In a bowl, combine 1 tablespoon of the oil with the turkey strips, lemon rind and juice, garlic and sage and set aside in the refrigerator to marinate for 5 minutes.

- Meanwhile, bring the vegetable stock to the boil in a pan and add the bulgar wheat. Cover and simmer for 7 minutes, then turn off the heat and set aside for about 10 minutes until the grains are tender and the liquid has been absorbed.

- Heat a frying pan with the remaining oil and scrape the marinated turkey into the pan. Stir-fry gently for about 10 minutes or until the turkey is cooked through. Fork gently into the cooked bulgar and spoon into dishes. Serve garnished with sage leaves, with steamed green beans or mangetout, if desired.

Sage, Lemon and Turkey Ciabatta

Place 125 g (4 oz) cream cheese in a bowl with 2 teaspoons finely chopped sage, 1 teaspoon each of finely grated lemon rind and juice, ½ small crushed garlic clove (optional) and a pinch each of salt and pepper. Mash with a fork until combined, then spread thickly over the cut bases of 2 ciabatta rolls. Top with about 125 g (4 oz) cooked, sliced turkey and fill each roll with a small handful of rocket or young spinach leaves. Serve cold or toast in a panini machine for 2–3 minutes until lightly toasted.

Sage and Lemon Baked Turkey

Steaks Mix 1 tablespoon olive or vegetable oil with the finely grated rind and juice of ½ lemon, 1 crushed garlic clove and 2 teaspoons shredded sage leaves in an ovenproof dish, then add 2 thick turkey steaks or turkey breast fillets, about 150 g (5 oz) each, and rub the marinade all over. Set aside in the refrigerator for 5 minutes. Heat another 1 tablespoon of olive or vegetable oil in a pan and cook the turkey steaks for about 2 minutes on each side until golden, then return to the ovenproof dish. Add 50 ml (2 fl oz) dry white wine, then cover with foil and bake in a preheated oven, 190°C (375°F), Gas Mark 5, for 15–20 minutes until the turkey is cooked but not dry, and the juices run clear when the meat is pierced with a skewer. Meanwhile, cook 150 g (5 oz) bulgar wheat in 325 ml (11 fl oz) vegetable stock as above. Spoon the bulgar onto warmed plates, top with the turkey and drizzle with the juices. Serve garnished with extra sage leaves and lemon wedges, if desired.

30 Wholewheat Pasta Bake with Blue Cheese and Walnuts

Serves 4

350 g (11½ oz) wholewheat penne or other pasta shape

1 head of broccoli, about 350 g (12 oz), broken into florets

2 tablespoons olive or vegetable oil

150 g (5 oz) shelled walnuts, chopped

3 spring onions, roughly sliced (optional)

2 teaspoons chopped sage or 1 teaspoon dried sage

150 ml (¼ pint) single cream

200 g (7 oz) soft blue cheese (such as dolcelatte, Gorgonzola or Saint Agur), diced

- Cook the pasta in a large pan of lightly salted boiling water for about 11 minutes until just tender. Add the broccoli for the final 3–4 minutes of cooking time. When the broccoli and pasta are just tender, drain well and return to the pan.

- Meanwhile, heat the oil in a frying pan and gently fry the walnuts and spring onions, if using, over a medium-low heat for 2–3 minutes, stirring frequently, until golden. Stir in the sage, cream and 150 g (5 oz) of the blue cheese until the cheese has melted and the sauce is creamy. Scrape into the drained pasta and broccoli, mix together, then tip the whole lot into an ovenproof dish.

- Scatter over the remaining cheese and bake in a preheated oven, 200°C (400°F), Gas Mark 6, for about 15 minutes until the topping is golden.

 Blue Cheese and Walnut Pasta Salad

Cook 400 g (13 oz) quick-cook pasta (such as fusilli or penne) in a pan of lightly salted boiling water for 3–5 minutes or according to the packet instructions until just tender. Cool under running cold water, drain and return to the pan. Stir in 3 tablespoons pesto with 2 teaspoons lemon juice and 2 tablespoons crème fraîche or soured cream. Spoon into bowls, then scatter over 150 g (5 oz) crumbled firm blue cheese (such as Stilton) and 75 g (3 oz) shelled walnut pieces to serve.

 Blue Cheese and Walnut Wholewheat Pasta Twists

Cook 400 g (13 oz) wholewheat fusilli in a large pan of lightly salted boiling water for about 11 minutes or according to the packet instructions until just tender. Meanwhile, heat 2 tablespoons olive or vegetable oil in a frying pan and cook 200 g (7 oz) sliced mushrooms over a medium heat for 5–6 minutes, stirring occasionally, until golden and tender. Add 2 chopped garlic cloves with 125 g (4 oz) shelled and chopped walnuts and 3 sliced spring onions and cook, stirring frequently, for 2–3 minutes. Pour in 150 ml (¼ pint) single cream and 150 g (5 oz) soft blue cheese and stir to melt. Remove from the heat and stir in 2 teaspoons lemon juice and a generous pinch each of salt and pepper. Drain the pasta, return to the pan and stir in the creamy mushroom and walnut sauce. Spoon the pasta into 4 warmed dishes and serve immediately.

1 ⏱ Sardine and Three Bean Salad

Serves 4

400 g (13 oz) can butter beans
  or cannellini beans, rinsed
  and drained
200 g (7 oz) canned kidney beans
  or black beans, rinsed and drained
300 g (10 oz) canned beans
  (such as broad beans or
  chickpeas), rinsed and drained
2 x 120 g (3¾ oz) cans sardines in
  oil or brine, drained and flaked
1 red onion, finely chopped
2 celery sticks, finely sliced
  (optional)
1 tablespoons red wine vinegar
3 tablespoons olive oil
salt and pepper

• Gently mix all of the ingredients together in a large
  bowl and season to taste.

• Spoon into bowls to serve.

Sardine and Bean Linguine

Heat 2 tablespoons olive oil in a frying pan and cook 1 finely chopped red onion, 2 finely chopped celery sticks and 2 finely chopped garlic cloves very gently for 10–12 minutes until softened but not coloured. Stir 2 x 120 g (3¾ oz) cans drained sardines and a 400 g (13 oz) can borlotti beans, rinsed and drained, into the pan and cook for 2–3 minutes until hot. Meanwhile, cook 400 g (13 oz) linguine or spaghetti in a large pan of lightly salted boiling water for about 11 minutes or according to the packet instructions until just tender. Drain the pasta, return it to the pan, then scrape the sardine mixture into the linguine and toss to combine. Heap into warmed dishes to serve.

Sardine and Brown Rice Bowl

Cook 300 g (10 oz) easy-cook brown rice in a pan of salted boiling water for 25 minutes until tender. Drain and rinse under cold water to cool. Meanwhile, in a large bowl, combine a 400 g (13 oz) can kidney beans, rinsed and drained, 1 chopped red pepper, 1 small chopped red onion, 2 tablespoons lime juice, 1 tablespoon light soy sauce, 2 tablespoons vegetable oil and 1 bunch chopped coriander. Fold through the cold rice and spoon into bowls. Scatter over 2 x 120 g (3¾ oz) cans drained and flaked sardines to serve.

STU-BRAI-FIQ

 # Spicy Chorizo and Tomato Pasta

Serves 4

2 tablespoons olive or
   vegetable oil
200 g (7 oz) chorizo sausage,
   diced
2 garlic cloves, chopped
2 x 400 g (13 oz) cans chopped
   tomatoes
½ teaspoon chilli flakes
150 g (5 oz) drained roasted
   peppers, roughly chopped
400 g (13 oz) pasta shapes
   (such as penne or fusilli)

- Heat the oil in a large frying pan or saucepan and cook the chorizo for 3–4 minutes until lightly golden. Add the remaining ingredients, except the pasta, and bring to the boil. Reduce the heat and simmer gently for 15 minutes, stirring occasionally, until rich and thickened.

- Meanwhile, cook the pasta in a large pan of lightly salted boiling water for about 11 minutes or according to the packet instructions until just tender. Drain and heap into dishes. Top with the spicy chorizo sauce to serve.

 Quick Fried Rice with Tomato and Chorizo Heat 2 tablespoons olive or vegetable oil in a frying pan and add 1 halved and thinly sliced red onion, 2 sliced garlic cloves, 1 deseeded and finely chopped red chilli (optional) and 200 g (7 oz) diced chorizo sausage. Cook over a medium-high heat for 3–4 minutes until slightly softened. Stir in 500 g (1 lb) cooked rice and 200 g (7 oz) defrosted or drained peas. Stir over the heat for 2–3 minutes until piping hot, then stir in 2 deseeded and diced tomatoes and spoon into warmed dishes to serve.

 One Pot Tomato and Chorizo Jambalaya Heat 2 tablespoons olive or vegetable oil in a large saucepan and cook 200 g (7 oz) diced chorizo sausage, 1 chopped red onion and 1 chopped red pepper over a medium-high heat for 4–5 minutes, stirring frequently, until slightly coloured. Stir in 1 tablespoon Cajun-style spice mix and 250 g (8 oz) rinsed long-grain rice, then add a 400 g (13 oz) can chopped tomatoes and 600 ml (1 pint) boiling stock. Bring to the boil, then reduce the heat, cover with a tight-fitting lid and simmer gently for about 20 minutes until the rice is tender and the liquid has been absorbed. Spoon into warmed dishes and serve with a few drops of Tabasco sauce and scattered with chopped parsley, if desired.

Carrot and Broccoli Vegetable Stir-Fry

Serves 2

1 tablespoon vegetable oil

250 g (8 oz) broccoli, cut into small florets

2 carrots, peeled and cut into thin batons

2 spring onions, cut into 2 cm (¾ inch) lengths

150 g (5 oz) mushrooms, halved or thickly sliced

175 g (6 oz) medium egg noodles

2 tablespoons sweet chilli sauce

1 tablespoon soy sauce, plus extra to serve

- Heat the oil in a large frying pan or wok and stir-fry the broccoli and carrot for 3 minutes over a medium-hot heat, until the vegetables begin to soften slightly.

- Add the spring onions and cook for a further 2 minutes until they are slightly coloured, then stir in the mushrooms. Stir-fry for 3–4 minutes until the mushrooms are just tender.

- Meanwhile, cook the noodles in a pan of boiling water for 3–4 minutes or according to the packet instructions until just tender, then drain.

- Remove the stir-fried vegetables from the heat, pour in the sweet chilli and soy sauce, then add the noodles and toss to coat. Heap into 2 warmed bowls and serve immediately with extra soy sauce, if desired.

Quick Broccoli and Carrot Couscous

Place 125 g (4 oz) couscous in a bowl with 25 g (1 oz) butter or 1 tablespoon olive or vegetable oil. Pour over 175 ml (6 fl oz) boiling hot vegetable stock and set aside for 5–7 minutes until the liquid has been absorbed and the grains are tender. Meanwhile, heat 2 tablespoons vegetable oil in a large wok and tip 400 g (13 oz) broccoli and carrot stir-fry medley into the pan. Stir-fry for 3–4 minutes until just tender but still slightly crunchy. Fold into the steamed couscous with 3 tablespoons sweet chilli sauce and serve immediately.

Crunchy Baked Carrots and

Broccoli Bring a large pan of lightly salted water to the boil. Cut 2 peeled carrots into batons and tip these into the water with 200 g (7 oz) each of broccoli and cauliflower florets. Cook the vegetables for 3–4 minutes until almost tender, then drain. Return to the pan and gently stir a 350 g (11½ oz) jar of tomato-based pasta sauce into the vegetables. Tip everything into an ovenproof dish and scatter over 2 slices of slightly stale bread, cubed. Top with 125 g (4 oz) grated cheese (such as Cheddar cheese or mozzarella) and cook in a preheated oven, 200°C (400°F), Gas Mark 6, for about 20 minutes until bubbling and crisp. Serve with green salad, if desired.

Red Cabbage and Beetroot Lentils

Serves 2

2 tablespoons olive or vegetable oil
½ small red cabbage, thinly sliced
2 spring onions, sliced, plus extra to garnish
1 beetroot, coarsely grated
1 teaspoon ground cumin
300 g (10 oz) canned green lentils, rinsed and drained
salt and pepper
natural or Greek yogurt, to serve

- Heat the oil in a saucepan and cook the red cabbage and spring onion over a medium heat for about 5 minutes until just beginning to soften. Stir in the beetroot, then cover and cook for a further 8–10 minutes, stirring occasionally, until the vegetables are tender.

- Sprinkle over the ground cumin and stir over the heat for a minute, then add the lentils and heat until hot. Season to taste, then spoon into 2 warmed dishes and serve with a dollop of yogurt and extra sliced spring onions.

 Red Cabbage Coleslaw

In a bowl, combine ½ small red cabbage with 1 small coarsely grated beetroot and 1 small peeled, cored and coarsely grated dessert apple. In a small bowl or jar, whisk 1 tablespoon wholegrain mustard with 1 finely chopped spring onion, 2 teaspoons red wine vinegar and 2 tablespoons olive oil. Pour over the vegetables and mix really well to coat. Serve with warmed wholemeal pittas.

 Fruity Braised Red Cabbage

Heat 2 tablespoons olive or vegetable oil in a saucepan and gently cook 1 finely chopped red onion over a a medium heat for 6–7 minutes until softened. Add 1 chopped garlic clove and 1 teaspoon ground cumin, then stir in half a shredded red cabbage, 1 peeled and coarsely grated dessert apple and a small handful of raisins. Cook gently for about 15 minutes, stirring frequently, until the vegetables are softened but still have some bite. Season to taste, then stir in 2 teaspoons balsamic vinegar and serve with grilled vegetarian sausages or sage and onion sausages.

STU-BRAI-LAA

10 Warm Bacon, Tomato and Butter Bean Salad

Serves 4

3 tablespoons olive or
   vegetable oil
6 back bacon rashers, chopped
2 garlic cloves, chopped
1 teaspoon paprika
3 tomatoes, deseeded and diced
2 x 400 g (13 oz) cans butter
   beans, rinsed and drained
2 tablespoons chopped parsley
2 tablespoons lemon juice

- Heat the oil in a large frying pan and cook the bacon over a medium heat for 6–7 minutes, stirring occasionally, until crisp and golden. Stir in the garlic and paprika for the final minute of cooking, then add the tomatoes, butter beans, parsley and lemon juice and toss to warm through.

- Spoon into 4 dishes and serve immediately.

2 Tomato, Bacon and Butter Bean Soup Heat the oil in a large saucepan and cook the bacon and 1 chopped onion for 7–8 minutes until lightly golden. Add 2 chopped garlic cloves and 1 teaspoon paprika for the final minute of cooking. Add a 400 g (13 oz) can butter beans, rinsed and drained, then 8 chopped sun-dried tomatoes, 500 g (1 lb) sieved tomatoes or passata and 500 ml (17 fl oz) hot ham or vegetable stock. Season with a generous pinch of pepper, then simmer for about 10 minutes. Use a hand-held blender to blend until smooth (alternatively, serve as a chunky soup), then ladle into warmed bowls to serve, scattered with a pinch of chopped parsley, if desired.

3 Tomato, Bacon and Butter Bean Stew Heat 3 tablespoons olive or vegetable oil in a large saucepan and cook 6 rashers of roughly chopped back bacon over a medium heat for 4–5 minutes until golden, then add 1 chopped onion and cook for a further 4–5 minutes until softened. Stir 2 large carrots, peeled and diced, 2 chopped garlic cloves and 1 teaspoon paprika into the pan and cook for 1–2 minutes until the garlic is softened. Add a 400 g (13 oz) can butter beans, rinsed and drained, a 400 g (13 oz) can chopped tomatoes and 250 ml (8 fl oz) hot vegetable stock. Bring to the boil, then cover, reduce the heat and simmer gently for about 15 minutes until thickened.

Scatter over 2 tablespoons chopped coriander and serve with couscous.

STU-BRAI-LOZ

30 Lime and Ginger Chicken Bowl

Serves 2

200 g (7 oz) chicken breast, sliced
175 g (6 oz) long-grain rice
125 g (4 oz) mangetout (optional)
lime wedges, to serve

For the marinade

1 tablespoon vegetable oil
2 tablespoons light soy sauce
2.5 cm (1 inch) piece of fresh root
   ginger, peeled and grated
1 garlic clove, peeled and grated

For the dressing

2.5 cm (1 inch) piece of fresh root
   ginger, peeled and grated
grated rind and juice of 2 limes
2 tablespoons light soy sauce
2 tablespoons vegetable oil
1 bunch of coriander, chopped

- Mix the chicken with the marinade ingredients and leave in the refrigerator to marinate for about 15 minutes.

- Cook the rice in a large pan of lightly salted boiling water for about 15 minutes or according to the packet instructions until just tender. Drain well and set aside to cool slightly.

- Meanwhile, combine the dressing ingredients and set aside. Place the mangetout in a small bowl with enough boiling water to cover. Set aside for 2–3 minutes until they are just tender but still have a slight crunch, then drain and set aside.

- Heat a dry frying pan and cook the marinated chicken gently for 10–12 minutes, stirring occasionally, until cooked through but not browned.

- Meanwhile, stir the dressing into the rice. Fold through the cooked chicken and mangetout and spoon into dishes to serve.

 Lime and Ginger Chicken Pot Noodle

Divide 150 g (5 oz) cooked straight-to-wok noodles between 2 bowls and top with 200 g (7 oz) cooked chicken, 1 teaspoon peeled and chopped fresh root ginger, 2 sliced spring onions, 100 g (3½ oz) shredded mangetout, 1 tablespoon soy sauce and 2 tablespoons lime juice. Pour 200 ml (7 fl oz) boiling vegetable stock into each bowl to cover the contents. Cover and set aside for 4–5 minutes until the noodles are tender. Serve immediately.

 Lime and Ginger Chicken Wrap

Mix 200 g (7 oz) sliced chicken breast with the marinade ingredients given above. Heat a dry frying pan and cook the chicken over a medium-high heat for 8–10 minutes until cooked through and lightly golden. Remove from the heat and set aside to cool slightly. Meanwhile, mix 2 tablespoons chopped coriander with 3 tablespoons mayonnaise and a pinch of black pepper. Spread the mayonnaise over 2 large or 4 small flour tortillas and scatter over a small handful of rocket, spinach or other salad leaves. Top with the chicken, then roll up tightly and serve immediately.

STU-BRAI-HEP

30 Beetroot, Mackerel and Goats' Cheese Lentils

Serves 4

200 g (7 oz) dried green lentils
3 tablespoons olive oil
2 red onions, finely sliced
125 ml (4 fl oz) balsamic vinegar
300 g (10 oz) cooked beetroot, rinsed and diced
2 x 125 g (4 oz) cans mackerel in oil or brine, drained and flaked
200 g (7 oz) firm goats' cheese, crumbled or diced
chopped chives, to garnish (optional)

- Cook the dried lentils a large pan of lightly salted boiling water for 15–18 minutes until tender but still holding their shape. Drain and set aside.

- Meanwhile, heat the oil in a large frying pan and cook the onion very gently for 12–15 minutes until really soft and golden. Pour the balsamic vinegar over the onion and simmer gently for 2–3 minutes until the vinegar begins to turn slightly syrupy.

- Remove from the heat and gently stir the lentils into the onion with the beetroot. Set aside to cool slightly for 4–5 minutes, then spoon into dishes and scatter over the flaked mackerel and crumbled goats' cheese. Garnish with chopped chives, if desired, to serve.

---

10 Beetroot Hummus with Mackerel

Rinse a 250 g (8 oz) vacuum pack of cooked beetroot, then roughly dice and place in a food processor with 2 tablespoons crème fraîche or natural yogurt, 1 tablespoon horseradish sauce (optional) and 1 tablespoon lemon juice. Process until smooth, then season to taste and spread thickly over toasted wholemeal pittas or granary toast. Drain and flake the mackerel from 2 x 125 g (4 oz) cans and serve garnished with chives, if desired.

20 Beetroot and Grilled Mackerel

Salad Cook 150 g (5 oz) dried green or Puy lentils in a large pan of lightly salted boiling water for 15–18 minutes until just tender. Drain and cool under cold water. (Alternatively, rinse and drain 400 g/13 oz canned green lentils.) Meanwhile, arrange 4 fresh mackerel fillets on the rack of a foil-lined grill tray, skin side up, and drizzle with 2 teaspoons oil. Cook under a grill preheated to a medium-high setting for 4–5 minutes on each side until just cooked.

Place 250 g (8 oz) cooked beetroot in a bowl with ½ finely chopped red onion (optional) and 1 tablespoon finely chopped chives. Drizzle over 2 tablespoons oil and 1 tablespoon red wine vinegar, then fold through the lentils and spoon onto 4 plates. Serve the salads topped with the roughly flaked grilled mackerel fillets.

Warm Sardine, Bean and Potato Salad

Serves 4

500 g (1 lb) new potatoes, halved or cut into bite-sized pieces

200 g (7 oz) fresh or frozen green beans

4 tablespoons olive or vegetable oil

1 red onion, thinly sliced

400 g (13 oz) can mixed bean salad or cannellini beans

2 x 120 g (3¾ oz) cans sardines in oil or brine, drained and flaked

1–2 tablespoons red or white wine or cider vinegar

rocket leaves, to serve (optional)

- Cook the potatoes in a large pan of lightly salted boiling water for about 15 minutes or until just tender. Add the green beans for the final 3–5 minutes of cooking – they should be just tender by the time the potatoes are done. Drain and set aside.

- Meanwhile, heat the oil in a frying pan and cook the red onion gently for 8–10 minutes until really tender and lightly golden. Stir in the mixed bean salad and heat gently for 2 minutes until warm. Remove from the heat and toss with the potatoes and flaked sardines, adding vinegar according to taste. Spoon into 4 dishes and serve immediately with rocket leaves, if desired.

Sardine and Bean Couscous

Place 250 g (8 oz) couscous and 25 g (1 oz) butter in a bowl, pour in 350 ml (12 fl oz) boiling vegetable stock or water, cover and set aside for 5–8 minutes until the liquid is absorbed. Meanwhile, pour a 400 g (13 oz) can mixed bean salad (not drained) into a pan and warm over a medium heat for 2–3 minutes. Take off the heat and stir in 2 x 120 g (3¾ oz) cans sardines, drained and flaked, 4 tablespoons oil and 1–2 tablespoons red or white wine vinegar. Fluff the couscous, then fold in the sardine mixture with 1 tablespoon harissa.

Sardine and Bean Bake

Heat 2 tablespoons olive or vegetable oil in a frying pan and cook 1 chopped red onion for 6–7 minutes until softened slightly. Stir in a 400 g (13 oz) can chopped tomatoes, 100 ml (3½ fl oz) water, a 400 g (13 oz) can kidney beans, rinsed and drained, a 400 g (13 oz) can cannellini beans, rinsed and drained, and ½ teaspoon mixed dried herbs (optional). Cover and simmer gently for 7–8 minutes until the beans are tender. Meanwhile, cut 1 small French stick into thick slices and spread each slice with 1 teaspoon pesto. Stir 2 x 120 g (3¾ oz) cans sardines, drained and flaked, into the beans and tip all of it into a buttered ovenproof dish. Top with the slices of French stick, pesto-side up, and scatter over 125 g (4 oz) grated cheese (such as Cheddar cheese or red Leicester). Place in a preheated oven, 220°C (425 °F), Gas Mark 7, for 12–15 minutes until the cheese has melted and is golden. Spoon into dishes and serve with a small rocket salad, if desired.

10 Spicy Peanut and Beef Wrap

Serves 2

200 g (7 oz) stir-fry beef strips

2 teaspoon Thai red curry paste

2 tablespoons vegetable oil

2 large soft tortilla wraps

75 g (3 oz) bean sprouts

2 small handfuls of shredded Iceberg lettuce

1½ tablespoons roasted peanuts, roughly chopped

2 lime quarters (optional)

- Place the beef in a bowl and mix thoroughly with the curry paste so that it is well coated.

- Heat the oil in a frying pan and cook the beef over a medium heat for 2–3 minutes until browned but still slightly pink.

- Meanwhile, fill the tortilla wraps with the bean sprouts and shredded lettuce. Top with the spicy beef strips, scatter over the chopped peanuts and squeeze over a little lime juice, if using. Roll up the wraps tightly to serve.

20 Beef Skewers with Satay Sauce

Mix 200 g (7 oz) diced beef with 2 teaspoons Thai red curry paste and 1 tablespoon coconut cream. Cut 1 red pepper and 1 onion into bite-sized pieces and thread onto skewers with the beef. Leave to marinate. Meanwhile, mix 3 tablespoons crunchy peanut butter with 1 teaspoon Thai red curry paste, 1 tablespoon lime juice and 3 tablespoons coconut cream. Warm gently to melt. Arrange the skewers on a grill rack. Cook under a medium-high grill for 8–10 minutes, turning occasionally, until tender. Leave to rest for 2 minutes. Serve with steamed rice, drizzled with warm satay sauce and garnished with coriander.

30 Beef and Bean Sprouts with

Peanuts Place a frying pan over a low heat and add a small handful of blanched peanuts. Cook over a low heat heat for 3–4 minutes until toasted. Tip onto a plate and return the pan to the heat. Add 2 tablespoons vegetable oil and cook 200 g (7 oz) stir-fry beef strips over a medium-high heat for 1–2 minutes until browned, then add 75 g (3 oz) bean sprouts and cook for 1 minute. Stir in 2 teaspoons Thai red curry paste, 200 ml (7 fl oz) coconut milk and 200 ml hot chicken or vegetable stock. Bring to the boil, then simmer gently for 5 minutes. Remove from the heat and stir in 2 tablespoons lime juice. Meanwhile, cook

125 g (4 oz) flat rice noodles in boiling water for about 3 minutes or according to the packet instructions until just tender. Heap the noodles into 2 deep bowls and ladle over the aromatic beef. Scatter with the toasted peanuts and a few chopped coriander leaves, if desired, to serve.

30 Spaghetti and Meatballs with Spicy Tomato Sauce

Serves 4

8 herby sausages, about 625 g
  (1¼ lb) total weight, or 20–24
  prepared meatballs
2 tablespoons olive or
  vegetable oil
1 onion, chopped or sliced
1 celery stick, trimmed
2 garlic cloves, crushed
½–1 teaspoon chilli flakes
500 g (1 lb) sieved tomatoes
  or passata
1 tablespoon tomato ketchup
400 g (13 oz) wholewheat
  spaghetti
salt and pepper

- If using sausages, squeeze the meat out of the casings and form into about 20 meatballs. Heat the oil in a saucepan and cook the meatballs over a medium heat for 6–7 minutes, turning occasionally, until golden. Remove with a slotted spoon and return the pan to the heat.

- Add the onion, celery and garlic to the pan and cook for 6–7 minutes until softened and lightly golden, then add the chilli flakes, passata and ketchup. Season lightly, cover and simmer for 12–15 minutes until thickened slightly. Return the meatballs to the pan for the final 7–8 minutes of cooking time until they are thoroughly cooked, then remove the pan from the heat.

- Meanwhile, cook the spaghetti in a large pan of lightly salted boiling water for 10–12 minutes or according to the packet instructions until just tender. Drain the pasta and heap into 4 warmed bowls, then top with the meatballs and sauce to serve.

 Spicy Tomato Meatball Stew

Heat 2 tablespoons olive or vegetable oil in a pan and cook 1 finely chopped red onion for 6–7 minutes until softened. Add 500 g (1 lb) cooked meatballs to the onion with 500 g (1 lb) tomato-based pasta sauce, 1 tablespoon harissa or Tabasco sauce and a 400 g (13 oz) can chickpeas, rinsed and drained. Bring to the boil, then simmer for 1–2 minutes until hot. Serve the meatball stew in bowls with couscous, if desired.

 Spicy Tomato Meatball Wraps

Place 500 g (1 lb) minced beef or turkey in a bowl with 30 g (1¼ oz) Mexican spice mix (such as fajita seasoning), 2 finely chopped spring onions, 1 crushed garlic clove and 1 teaspoon dried oregano. Season and mix really well with your hands, then form into 20 meatballs. Heat 2 tablespoons olive or vegetable oil in a frying pan and cook the meatballs over a medium heat for 12–14 minutes, turning occasionally, until golden and cooked through. Meanwhile, warm 250 g (8 oz) cooked rice, then divide it between 4 large soft tortilla wraps. Top with 150 g (5 oz) grated Cheddar cheese and a generous dollop of spicy tomato salsa. Arrange the meatballs over the spicy tomato sauce, then roll up and wrap each one in foil. Cook in a preheated oven, 200°C (400°F), Gas Mark 6, for 3–4 minutes until the wraps are soft and warm. Serve from the foil with shredded Iceberg lettuce, if desired.

STU-BRAI-GEZ

30 Lemony Salmon Goujons

Serves 2

1 large sweet potato, cut into
wedges

5 tablespoons olive or vegetable
oil, plus extra for frying

2 tablespoons plain flour

1 egg, beaten

50 g (2 oz) fresh or dried
breadcrumbs

2 teaspoons finely grated
lemon rind

250 g (8 oz) salmon or other
boneless fish fillet, cut into
thick, chunky strips

salt and pepper

To serve (optional)

green salad or vegetables
lemon wedges

- Toss the sweet potato wedges in a bowl with 2 tablespoons of the oil and a pinch each of salt and pepper. Tip onto a baking sheet and bake in a preheated oven, 200°C (400°F), Gas Mark 6, for about 25 minutes, turning occasionally, until tender and golden.

- Meanwhile, place the flour, egg and breadcrumbs in 3 separate dishes. Mix the lemon rind into the breadcrumbs. Season the flour with a pinch each of salt and pepper and dust the pieces of salmon to coat. Dip the fish pieces, one by one, first into the seasoned flour, then into the beaten egg, then into the breadcrumbs, turning to coat completely.

- Heat the remaining oil in a large non-stick frying pan and cook the goujons for about 3 minutes on each side until they are golden and crispy and the salmon is flaky. Remove, drain on kitchen paper and keep warm.

- Serve the goujons with the potato wedges and green salad or vegetables and lemon wedges, if desired.

---

10 Smoked Salmon with Lemon Mayo

Mix 2 tablespoons mayonnaise with 1 teaspoon lemon juice and spread evenly over 4 slices of brown or granary bread. Top each with a small handful of baby spinach leaves, then divide 120 g (3¾ oz) smoked salmon trimmings or 4 large slices of smoked salmon on top. Season generously with black pepper and serve with a squeeze of lemon juice, if desired.

20 Simple Grilled Salmon with Horseradish Mash

Cook 2 large peeled potatoes, cut into chunks, in a large pan of lightly salted boiling water for 12–15 minutes until tender. Rub 1 teaspoon oil over 2 chunky salmon fillets and place on the rack of a foil-lined grill tray. Season with a pinch of pepper and cook under a grill preheated to a medium-high setting for 4–6 minutes on each side or until cooked but still slightly pink in the middle. Drain the potatoes, then return to the pan with 1 heaped tablespoon horseradish sauce, 25 g (1 oz) butter and a splash of milk. Mash until smooth, then spoon onto 2 warmed plates. Top with the salmon and serve immediately with steamed spinach, if desired, and lemon wedges.

STU-BRAI-TAG

QuickCook
Chilled-Out
TV Dinners

Recipes listed by cooking time

30

Piri Piri Sausage Bake   128

Tuna and Olive
Bean Burgers   130

One-Pot Garlicky
Tomato Rice   132

Hoi Sin Baked Mushrooms
with Rice   134

Creamy Fish Pie   136

Vegetable Bulgar Pilau   138

Chunky Spiced Bean
Soup   140

Honey-Mustard Sausages
with Potato Wedges   142

Potato and Onion Pasties 144

Soy Chicken with Rice   146

Potato, Cauliflower and
Spinach Curry   148

Lazy Bacon, Pea and
Courgette Risotto   150

Wholewheat Pasta Bake
with Anchovies   152

Cheesy Tuna Puffs   154

Lemony Baked
Fish Parcels   156

Mint, Red Onion and
Feta Rice Salad   158

Stove-Top Chorizo Pizza 160

Jalepeño Turkey Chilli   162

Veggie Soupy Noodles   164

Chilli Pea and Pulse
Korma   166

Sweet and Sour Pork   168

Garlicky Macaroni Cheese 170

Chorizo and Bean Stew   172

Beef and Onion Stew   174

20

Piri Piri Sausage and Beans 128

Tuna and Olive Pasta   130

Simple Tomato and
Garlic Sauce for Pasta   132

Mushrooms in Black
Bean Sauce   134

Creamy Fish with Mash   136

Steamed Bulgar with
Grilled Vegetables   138

Spicy Bean Quesadilla   140

Herby Sausages with
Honey-Mustard Dip   142

Potato and Onion
Omelette   144

Soy Noodles with Chicken 146

Cauliflower, Chickpea and
Spinach Curry   148

Lazy One-Pot Pea and
Bacon Pasta   150

Wholewheat Spaghetti with
Tomatoes and Anchovies 152

Tuna Gnocchi Bake   154

Lemon Butter Fried Fish 156

Minty Pea, Red Onion and
Feta Omelette with Salad 158

10

Oven-Baked
Chorizo Pizza 160

Jalepeño Turkey Burgers 162

Bowl of Veggie Noodles 164

Chilli Pea Soup 166

Sweet Chilli Pork
Stir-Fry 168

Garlicky Spaghetti
Carbonara 170

Chorizo and Beans
with Penne 172

Beef and Crispy Onion
Burgers 174

Piri Piri Hot-Dog 128

Tuna and Olive Salad 130

Quick Garlicky
Tomato Lentils 132

Mushroom and Egg-
Fried Rice 134

Creamy Prawn Spaghetti 136

Vegetable Couscous 138

Spicy Bean Tostada 140

Honey-Mustard
Sausage Roll 142

Cheese and Onion
Potato Waffles 144

Soy Chicken and
Rice Noodles 146

Curried Cauliflower
Lentils on Toast 148

Lazy Pea and Bacon
Noodles 150

Quick-Cook Pasta with
Chillies and Anchovies 152

Cheesy Tuna Rarebit 154

Lemony Fish Pâté
on Toast 156

Minted Potato, Red Onion
and Feta Salad 158

Under-The-Grill
Chorizo Pizza 160

Jalepeño Turkey Melt 162

Veggie Noodle Salad 164

Chilli Pea Pasta 166

Sweet and Sour
Pork Noodles 168

Spaghetti with Garlic
and Black Pepper 170

Chorizo'd Bowl of
Baked Beans 172

Beef and Onion Wraps 174

1 Piri Piri Hot-Dog

Serves 4

2 tablespoons vegetable oil
1 red onion, thinly sliced
1 red pepper, thinly sliced
4 teaspoon piri piri seasoning mix
  or medium chilli powder
1 tablespoon lemon juice or water
8 cooked sausages or
  Frankfurters
4–8 hot dog buns, split
creamy coleslaw, to serve
  (optional)

- Heat the oil in a large frying pan and cook the onion and pepper over a high heat for 5–6 minutes until coloured.

- Reduce the heat and tip the piri piri seasoning mix, lemon juice or water and sausages into the pan. Cook the sausages and spices for 2–3 minutes, shaking the pan frequently to cook evenly.

- Arrange the piri piri sausages in their hot dog buns and serve immediately with creamy coleslaw.

2 Piri Piri Sausage and Beans

Cut 6 pork sausages into 2.5 cm (1 inch) chunks. Heat 2 tablespoons olive or vegetable oil in a large frying pan and cook the sausage pieces over a medium heat with 1 finely chopped onion and 1 finely chopped red pepper for about 8 minutes until the vegetables are softened. Add 3 teaspoons piri piri seasoning mix and cook for a further 2 minutes, stirring frequently. Pour 500 g (1 lb) sieved tomatoes or passata into the pan with 2 x 400 g (13 oz) cans beans (such as butter beans, haricot or cannellini beans) and simmer gently for 7–8 minutes until the beans are tender and the sauce is rich and thick. Serve with toast or with baked potatoes for a more substantial meal.

3 Piri Piri Sausage Bake

Place 8 of your preferred sausages in a large roasting tin with 1 large onion and 2 red peppers that have been cut into thin wedges. Toss with 3 tablespoons vegetable oil, 1 tablespoon lemon juice and 4 teaspoons piri piri seasoning mix, then bake in a preheated oven, 200°C (400°F), Gas Mark 6, for 20–25 minutes, turning occasionally, until the sausages are cooked through. Serve with crusty bread and creamy coleslaw.

 Tuna and Olive Pasta

Serves 2 as a light lunch or snack or 4 as a small starter

3 tablespoons olive or vegetable oil

1 red onion, sliced

2 garlic cloves, chopped

2 x 400 g (13 oz) cans chopped tomatoes

½ teaspoon chilli flakes (optional)

400 g (13 oz) pasta shapes (such as penne)

185 g (6½ oz) can tuna in brine or oil, drained and flaked

75 g (3 oz) pitted black or green olives, drained and roughly chopped

- Heat the oil in a large frying pan or saucepan and cook the onion over a medium heat for 6–7 minutes until it begins to soften. Add the garlic and cook for a further minute. Pour the chopped tomatoes into the pan with the chilli flakes, if using. Simmer gently for 8–10 minutes until thickened slightly.

- Meanwhile, bring a large pan of lightly salted water to the boil and cook the pasta for 10–12 minutes or according to the packet instructions until just tender. Drain and return to the pan. Stir the sauce into the pasta with the tuna and olives and heap into 4 warmed dishes to serve.

 Tuna and Olive Salad

Lower 4 small eggs into a pan of boiling water and simmer gently for 6–7 minutes. Meanwhile, shred 1 small Iceberg lettuce, cut 2 tomatoes into wedges and flake the drained tuna from a 185 g (6½ oz) can. Arrange the salad on 4 plates and scatter over 75 g (3 oz) pitted black or green olives and 100 g (3½ oz) herby croutons (optional). Cool the eggs under cold running water, then peel. Cut into quarters and arrange on top of each salad. Serve immediately with French-style vinaigrette.

 Tuna and Olive Bean Burgers

Drain a 400 g (13 oz) can haricot beans and place in a bowl. Mash the beans with the back of a fork or a potato masher to crush, then add a 185 g (6½ oz) can tuna, drained, 50 g (2 oz) finely chopped pitted green olives, 100 g (3½ oz) drained sweetcorn, 2 finely chopped spring onions, 1 small beaten egg and 1 tablespoon chopped chives (optional). Mash together really well, then season with a little salt and pepper and form into 4 large patties. Dust with a little flour or dried breadcrumbs and chill for

about 15 minutes to firm up slightly. Shallow-fry over a medium heat in a large frying pan for 2–3 minutes on each side until golden. Arrange on 4 burger buns with your desired fillings (such as a slice of Cheddar cheese or red Leicester cheese, slices of tomatoes and a couple of lettuce leaves). Top with ketchup, mayonnaise or tartare sauce and serve immediately.

10 Quick Garlicky Tomato Lentils

Serves 4

2 tablespoons olive or
   vegetable oil
1 large onion, chopped
2 garlic cloves, chopped
440 g (14¼ oz) jar tomato-based
   pasta sauce
1 teaspoon dried oregano or
   mixed herbs (optional)
2 x 390 g (12½ oz) cans green
   lentils, drained
100 g (3½ oz) grated Cheddar
   cheese, Parmesan cheese or
   other hard Italian cheese
   (optional)
crusty bread or toast, to serve
   (optional)

- Heat the oil in a large frying pan and cook the onion and garlic over a medium heat for 6–7 minutes, stirring frequently, until softened. Add the pasta sauce, dried oregano or mixed herbs, if using, and lentils and heat to simmering point.

- Spoon into bowls. Scatter with cheese, if using, and serve immediately with crusty bread or toast, if desired.

---

20 Simple Tomato and Garlic Sauce for Pasta Heat the oil in a large frying pan or saucepan and cook the onion and garlic over a medium heat for 6–7 minutes, as above. Pour 2 x 400 g (13 oz) cans chopped or plum tomatoes into the pan with the dried oregano or mixed herbs, if using. Simmer gently for 10–12 minutes, stirring occasionally, until thickened slightly, then spoon over cooked pasta or baked potatoes. Sprinkle with grated cheese to serve, if desired.

30 One-Pot Garlicky Tomato Rice Heat 2 tablespoons olive or vegetable oil in a large saucepan and cook 1 large chopped onion and 1 chopped red, green or yellow pepper for 6–7 minutes until they begin to soften. Add 2 chopped garlic cloves and cook for a further minute, then stir in 250 g (8oz) long-grain white rice. Add 2 x 400 g (13 oz) cans chopped tomatoes, 1 teaspoon dried oregano or mixed herbs, 450 ml (¾ pint) boiling water and 1 crumbled vegetable stock cube. Stir well to combine, then reduce the heat, cover with a lid and simmer gently for 18–20 minutes until the rice is tender and most of the liquid has been absorbed. Spoon into bowls and serve with a hot chilli sauce, if desired.

Mushroom and Egg-Fried Rice

Serves 2

2 tablespoons vegetable oil

200 g (7 oz) mushrooms, chopped

2 spring onions

1 large egg, beaten

250 g (8 oz) cooked rice

soy sauce, to serve

- Heat the oil in a large frying pan and add the mushrooms and spring onion. Stir-fry over a medium heat for 4–5 minutes until the mushrooms have softened.

- Increase the heat and add the beaten egg to the pan. Cook for a further 2 minutes, stirring frequently, until the egg is cooked. Stir in the rice and heat until it is really hot, then remove from the heat and spoon the mixture into bowls.

- Serve immediately with soy sauce.

2 Mushrooms in Black Bean Sauce

Heat 2 tablespoons vegetable oil in a large frying pan or wok and add 1 large sliced onion and 1 sliced green pepper. Stir-fry over a medium-hot heat for 3–4 minutes until lightly coloured. Add 150 g (5 oz) halved mushrooms and 1 sliced garlic clove (optional) and stir-fry for a further 4–5 minutes until softened and lightly coloured. Pour in a jar of black bean or sweet-and-sour cook-in sauce weighing about 200 g (7 oz) and simmer gently for 3–4 minutes. Remove from the heat and serve immediately with cooked noodles or rice.

3 Hoi Sin Baked Mushrooms with Rice

Arrange 8–10 large flat mushrooms in a large ovenproof dish, stalk-side up. In a small dish, mix 2 teaspoons peeled and grated fresh root ginger (optional) in a dish with 1 crushed garlic clove, 2 tablespoons vegetable oil and 3 tablespoons hoi sin or black bean stir-fry sauce. Drizzle this mixture over the mushrooms, then cover with kitchen foil and bake in a preheated oven, 180°C (350°F), Gas Mark 4, for 15–20 minutes until the mushrooms are softened and aromatic. Meanwhile, rinse 150 g (5 oz) long-grain white rice under running water and cook in a large pan of lightly salted boiling water for 12–15 minutes or according to the packet instructions until just tender. Drain well and spoon into dishes. Top each bowl of rice with 4–5 mushrooms and drizzle with juices to serve.

STU-CHIL-XIT

30 Creamy Fish Pie

Serves 4

350 g (11½ oz) cheese pasta sauce

350 g (11½ oz) mixed fish (such as salmon, haddock and pollack), cut into chunks

125 g (4 oz) frozen peeled prawns (optional)

200 g (7 oz) mixture of frozen peas and sweetcorn

2 tablespoons chopped parsley or chives

500 g (1 lb) leftover mashed potato

100 g (3½ oz) grated cheese (such as Cheddar cheese or Red Leicester)

sliced green beans or salad, to serve

- Place the cheese sauce in a saucepan and heat gently until almost bubbling. Stir through the mixed fish for 2–3 minutes until almost cooked through.
- Stir in the frozen prawns, if using, with the vegetables and bring to almost boiling point. Remove from the heat and stir through the herbs.
- Scrape the pie filling into a medium-sized ovenproof dish, then top evenly with the mashed potato and sprinkle with the grated cheese.
- Bake in a preheated oven, 200°C (400°F), Gas Mark 7, for about 20 minutes until bubbling and golden. Serve immediately with sliced green beans or salad.

Creamy Prawn Spaghetti

Cook 400 g (13 oz) quick-cook spaghetti in a pan of lightly salted boiling water for 4–5 minutes until just tender. Meanwhile, heat 25 g (1 oz) butter in a pan and add 3 sliced spring onions. Cook over a medium heat for 2–3 minutes. Add 300 g (10 oz) cream cheese with chives and warm gently to melt. Stir in 250 g (8 oz) cooked peeled prawns and warm gently for 2–3 minutes until hot. Drain the pasta, return to the pan and stir through the creamy prawns. Serve immediately, sprinkled with chopped parsley or chives.

Creamy Fish with Mash

Arrange 4 chunky fish fillets (such as pollack, coley or salmon) in a medium-sized ovenproof dish. Pour over 350 g (11½ oz) warmed cheese pasta sauce and sprinkle over 100 g (3½ oz) grated cheese (such as Cheddar cheese or red Leicester). Bake in a preheated oven, 200°C (400°C), Gas Mark 6, for 15–18 minutes until the fish is flaky. Meanwhile, cook 750 g (1½ lb) peeled potatoes in a large pan of lightly salted boiling water for 12–15 minutes until tender. Drain, return to the pan with 50 g (2 oz) butter, 3 tablespoons milk and a pinch each of salt and pepper. Mash with a potato masher until smooth. Serve the baked fish with the mashed potato and some sliced green beans.

Steamed Bulgar with Grilled Vegetables

Serves 4

250 g (8 oz) bulgar wheat
600 ml (1 pint) vegetable stock
  or boiling water
2 red or green peppers, cut into
  bite-sized pieces
2 courgettes, cut into bite-sized
  pieces
1 large onion, cut into bite-sized
  pieces
200 g (7 oz) mushrooms, halved
olive, vegetable or flavoured oil
  (such as chilli oil), for drizzling
tzatziki or minty yogurt dip, to
  serve (optional)

- Pour the bulgar wheat into a large pan and pour over the stock or boiling water. Heat until simmering and simmer gently, covered, for 7 minutes. Set aside until the liquid has been absorbed.

- Meanwhile, thread the pieces of vegetables onto 4 long or 8 short metal skewers, then drizzle with a little oil and arrange on the rack of a foil-lined grill tray or a foil-covered baking sheet. Cook under grill preheated to a medium-hot setting for 15–18 minutes, turning occasionally, until the vegetables are just tender and lightly charred.

- Spoon the steamed bulgar into dishes and serve alongside the veggie skewers. Serve with a dish of tzatziki or minty yogurt dip, if desired.

Vegetable Couscous

Place 250 g (8 oz) couscous in a bowl with a 25 g (1 oz) knob of butter and pour over 300 ml (½ pint) boiling vegetable stock or water. Cover and set aside for 5–8 minutes until the liquid has been absorbed and the grains are tender. Meanwhile, finely chop 1 small red onion, peel and coarsely grate 2 carrots and dice 500 g (1 lb) cooked beetroot. Fold the vegetables into the tender couscous with 2 tablespoons vinaigrette dressing and serve immediately.

Vegetable Bulgar Pilau

Heat 2 tablespoons vegetable or olive oil in a large deep-sided frying pan and add 1 large chopped onion, 1 chopped red or green pepper (optional) and 2 garlic cloves, chopped. Cook over a medium heat for 6–7 minutes until the vegetables begin to soften. Stir in 250 g (8 oz) bulgar wheat until the grains are coated in oil. Stir in 300 g (10 oz) fresh, frozen or leftover mixed chopped vegetables or peas. Pour in 600 ml (1 pint) boiling vegetable stock or boiling water with a stock cube, then reduce the heat, cover and simmer gently for 10–15 minutes until the liquid has been absorbed and the grains are tender. Spoon into bowls and serve scattered with chopped parsley, if desired.

STU-CHIL-ZIQ

30 Chunky Spiced Bean Soup

Serves 4

2 tablespoons vegetable or
  olive oil

1 large onion, chopped

1 red pepper, chopped

1 red chilli, deseeded and chopped

2 garlic cloves, chopped (optional)

400 g (13 oz) can mixed beans,
  rinsed and drained

500 g (1 lb) passata or sieved
  tomatoes

750 ml (1¼ pints) hot vegetable
  stock

200 g (7 oz) mixed chopped
  frozen or leftover vegetables

salt and pepper

roughly chopped parsley, to serve
  (optional)

- Heat the oil in a large saucepan and add the onion, pepper, chilli and garlic, if using. Cook gently over a medium heat for 6–7 minutes until softened. Stir in the beans, passata and stock and bring to the boil. Reduce the heat slightly and simmer gently for 12–15 minutes until thickened slightly.

- Add the vegetables and simmer gently for a further 3–4 minutes until just tender. Season to taste, then ladle into bowls and serve hot, sprinkled with roughly chopped parsley, if desired.

---

10 Spicy Bean Tostada

Heat a large frying pan and toast 4 large soft flour tortillas for 30–60 seconds on each side until crisp and lightly golden. Arrange on serving plates and spread a 400 g (13 oz) can refried beans, warmed, over the tortillas. Scatter each tortilla with 1 chopped tomato and 1 chopped spring onion. Deseed and finely chop 1 large red chilli, then scatter over the tostadas. Alternatively, drizzle over a few drops of Tabasco or other hot chilli sauce. Serve immediately with shredded Iceberg lettuce and a dollop of soured cream, if desired.

20 Spicy Bean Quesadilla

Heat 2 tablespoons vegetable oil in a frying pan and cook the onion, pepper and chilli as above for 6–7 minutes until softened. Add a 400 g (13 oz) can mixed beans, haricot or kidney beans and 200 ml (7 fl oz) hot vegetable stock and simmer for 4–5 minutes until slightly softened. Mash the beans using the back of a fork, then spread the chunky mixture over 4 medium-sized flour tortillas. Scatter each with 25 g (1 oz) grated cheese (such as Cheddar cheese or Emmental), then top with a second tortilla. Toast each quesadilla for 30–60 seconds on each side in a large dry frying pan until the tortillas are lightly toasted and the cheese is melting. Serve immediately with shredded Iceberg lettuce and a dollop of soured cream, if desired.

Honey-Mustard Sausages with Potato Wedges

Serves 4

1 kg (2 lb) new potatoes,
  cut into wedges
4 tablespoons vegetable oil
1 teaspoon dried thyme (optional)
12 thin pork sausages
2 tablespoons clear honey
2 tablespoons wholegrain
  mustard
salt and pepper
green salad and/or coleslaw,
  to serve (optional)

- Toss the potato wedges with 2 tablespoons of the oil, the thyme and a pinch each of salt and pepper. Tip onto a large baking sheet and bake in a preheated oven, 200°C (400°F), Gas Mark 6, for about 25 minutes, turning occasionally, until tender and golden.

- While the potatoes are cooking, place the sausages on a small baking sheet or in a roasting tin or ovenproof dish. Drizzle over the remaining oil and cook in the oven for about 20 minutes, turning occasionally, until cooked and golden.

- Meanwhile, mix together the honey and mustard. After 20 minutes, remove the sausages from the oven and pour over the honey-mustard mixture. Turn to coat, then return to the oven for 4–5 minutes until sticky.

- Remove the sausages from the oven and cool slightly before serving with the potato wedges and plenty of green salad and/or coleslaw, if desired.

---

1 **Honey-Mustard Sausage Roll**

In a small bowl, mix 1 teaspoon clear honey and 2 teaspoons wholegrain mustard with 6 tablespoons mayonnaise. Cut open 4 mini baguettes or similar crusty bread rolls and spread the mayonnaise thickly over the cut sides. Top with 8 sliced pork or chicken Frankfurters (or use leftover cooked sausages) and a small handful of green salad, if desired. Serve immediately.

2 **Herby Sausages with Honey- Mustard Dip** Arrange 12 thin pork sausages on the rack of a foil-lined grill tray. Cook under a grill preheated to a medium setting for 12–18 minutes or according to the packet instructions, turning frequently, until golden brown and cooked through. Meanwhile, place 3 tablespoons clear honey and 3 tablespoons wholegrain mustard in a small pan with

½ teaspoon dried thyme, if desired. Heat gently until the dipping sauce is runny and warm. Pour into a small bowl and serve with the hot sausages.

10 Cheese and Onion Potato Waffles

Serves 2

4 frozen potato waffles

2 tablespoons vegetable or olive oil

4 spring onions, sliced

1 teaspoon dried thyme (optional)

125 g (4 oz) grated mature cheese (such as Cheddar cheese, red Leicester or double Gloucester)

pepper

green salad, to serve

- Arrange the potato waffles on a grill rack and cook under a grill preheated to a medium setting for 6–8 minutes, turning once, or according to the packet instructions, until hot and golden.

- Meanwhile, heat the oil in a medium-sized frying pan and cook the spring onion over a medium heat for 3–4 minutes until softened. Stir in the dried thyme and set aside to cool slightly before mixing with the grated cheese and plenty of pepper.

- Leaving the waffles on the grill tray, scatter over the cheese mixture, then return the tray to the grill for a further minute until the cheese has melted. Serve with green salad.

20 Potato and Onion Omelette

Heat 2 tablespoons olive or vegetable oil in a frying pan and add 1 large thinly sliced onion. Cook over a medium heat for 7–8 minutes, stirring occasionally. Slice 200 g (7 oz) drained canned potatoes and add to the pan with 1 teaspoon dried thyme. Lightly beat 5 eggs, season, and pour into the pan. Cook gently for 5–6 minutes until the egg is just firm, then scatter over 100 g (3½ oz) grated Cheddar cheese, red Leicester or double Gloucester. Cook under a grill preheated to a medium-hot setting for 2–3 minutes until the cheese is melted and lightly browned. Cut into wedges and serve with green salad.

30 Potato and Onion Pasties

Dice 200 g (7 oz) cooked leftover potatoes or drained canned potatoes and place in a bowl with 2 finely chopped spring onions and 125 g (4 oz) crumbled cheese (try Wensleydale, feta or Stilton). Add ½ teaspoon dried thyme (optional) and a generous pinch of black pepper. Unroll a 325 g (11 oz) sheet of short-crust pastry and cut out 2 x 18 cm (7 inch) circles. Spread about 1–2 tablespoons onion chutney (optional) over each circle, keeping the chutney away from the edge. Now divide the cheese-and-potato filling between each pastry and brush a 1 cm (½ in) border around the edge with a little beaten egg or milk. Fold over the pastry to encase the filling, crimping the edges together to seal and create 2 pasties. Arrange on baking sheets, then brush with a little extra milk or beaten egg and bake in a preheated oven, 200°C (400°F), Gas Mark 6, for 15–20 minutes until golden. Serve warm with green salad or vegetables.

1 Soy Chicken and Rice Noodles

Serves 2

300 g (10 oz) packet of
cooked rice noodles

2 tablespoons soy sauce

1 tablespoon sesame or
vegetable oil

½ red chilli, deseeded and finely
sliced or chopped (optional)

1 teaspoon peeled and grated
fresh root ginger

150 g (5 oz) cooked chicken
breast, sliced or torn

2 spring onions, sliced

1 red pepper or 125 g (4 oz)
mangetout, thinly sliced

- Place the noodles in a sieve or colander and pour a kettleful of boiling water over them. Drain, then cool under running cold water. Drain well and place in a large bowl.

- Whisk together the soy sauce, oil, chilli and ginger and drizzle the mixture over the noodles. Toss really well to coat, then add the remaining ingredients and mix gently to combine. Heap into bowls to serve.

---

2 Soy Noodles with Chicken

Heat 2 tablespoons vegetable oil in a frying pan and cook 1 large, thinly sliced chicken breast over a medium-high heat for 5–6 minutes until lightly golden and just cooked through. Add 125 g (4 oz) sliced mangetout, 2 sliced spring onions, a 1.5 cm (¾ inch) piece of fresh root ginger, peeled and chopped, 2 sliced garlic cloves and ½ chopped red chilli. Stir-fry for 2–3 minutes until softened, then add 300 g (10 oz) straight-to-wok noodles and stir-fry for 3 minutes until hot. Pour in 2 tablespoons light soy sauce and 2 tablespoons oyster sauce, toss to coat and heap into bowls.

3 Soy Chicken with Rice

Heat 2 tablespoons vegetable oil in a frying pan and cook 4 boned chicken thighs, skin side down, over a medium-high heat for 6–8 minutes until golden and crispy. Turn and cook the other side for 4–6 minutes until the chicken is cooked through. Remove from the pan and set aside. Meanwhile, cook 200 g (7 oz) medium egg noodles in a pan of boiling water for about 4 minutes or according to the packet instructions until tender. Return the pan that contained the chicken to a low heat, add a little more oil if necessary, and add 2 thickly sliced spring onions, a 1.5 cm (¾ inch) piece

of fresh root ginger, peeled and chopped, 2 sliced garlic cloves and half a chopped red chilli (optional) to the pan. Stir-fry gently for 2–3 minutes until softened, then add 1 large handful of bean sprouts and cook for a further 2 minutes until slightly softened. Pour in 3 tablespoons light soy sauce, 1 tablespoon clear honey and 2 tablespoons water. Return the chicken to the pan for 3–4 minutes until hot and slightly sticky. Serve with steamed rice.

STU-CHIL-HIP

30 Potato, Cauliflower and Spinach Curry

Serves 4

3 tablespoons vegetable oil

450 g (14½ oz) potatoes, peeled and cut into bite-sized chunks

1 large onion, roughly chopped

4 tablespoons medium curry paste (such as bhuna, balti or jalfrezi paste)

½ small cauliflower, about 250 g (8 oz) in weight, cut into chunky florets

300 ml (½ pint) hot vegetable or chicken stock

200 ml (7 fl oz) coconut milk

150 g (5 oz) frozen leaf spinach

To serve

cooked rice or warmed naan bread

chopped coriander (optional)

- Heat the oil in a large deep-sided frying pan or saucepan and cook the potato and onion over a medium heat for 5–6 minutes, stirring occasionally, until the vegetables are tinged with colour and begin to soften. Stir in the curry paste and cook for 1 minute to cook the spices.

- Tip the cauliflower into the pan and stir to coat before adding the hot stock and coconut milk. Bring to the boil, then reduce the heat, cover and simmer gently for about 15 minutes, stirring occasionally, until the potatoes and cauliflower are tender and the sauce has thickened.

- Stir in the frozen spinach and cook for a further 2–3 minutes until the spinach has wilted and the curry is hot. Serve spooned over bowls of rice or with warmed naan and sprinkled with chopped coriander, if desired.

10 Curried Cauliflower Lentils on Toast

Boil 250 g (8 oz) cauliflower florets for 5–6 minutes until just tender, then drain. Meanwhile, heat 2 tablespoons vegetable oil in a large pan and cook 1 large chopped onion over a medium heat for 6–7 minutes until almost softened. Stir a 500 g (1 lb) jar of mild curry sauce into the onion with a 390 g (12½ oz) can green lentils, rinsed and drained, and the cauliflower. Stir over the heat for 1–2 minutes until hot, then spoon over slices of hot buttered toast to serve.

20 Cauliflower, Chickpea and Spinach Curry

Heat 2 tablespoons vegetable oil in a large frying pan or saucepan and cook 1 finely chopped onion over a medium-high heat for 5–6 minutes until coloured and beginning to soften. Stir in 3 tablespoons medium curry paste and cook for 1 minute, then stir in 325 g (11 oz) cauliflower florets, 6 roughly chopped tomatoes, a 400 g (13 oz) can chickpeas, rinsed and drained, and 400 ml (14 fl oz) hot vegetable stock or water. Bring to the boil, then reduce the heat and simmer gently for about 10 minutes, adding a little extra liquid if necessary, until the cauliflower is tender and the sauce has thickened slightly. Stir in 200 g (7 oz) washed spinach leaves and cook for 1 minute until they have just wilted, then spoon the curry into bowls and serve immediately with warmed naan bread, if desired.

30 Lazy Bacon, Pea and Courgette Risotto

Serves 4

50 g (2 oz) butter
150 g (5 oz) streaky bacon, diced
300 g (10 oz) risotto rice
100 ml (3½ fl oz) dry white wine (optional)
900 ml (1½ pints) hot chicken or vegetable stock (add an extra 100 ml/3½ fl oz if not using wine)
2 courgettes, about 325 g (11 oz) total weight, coarsely grated
200 g (7 oz) frozen peas, defrosted
1 small bunch of basil, shredded (optional)
salt and pepper
grated Parmesan cheese, to serve (optional)

- Melt the butter in a large frying pan or saucepan and cook the diced bacon over a medium heat for 6–7 minutes until golden. Remove half of the bacon with a slotted spoon and set aside.

- Stir in the risotto rice and pour in the white wine, if using, and hot stock. Bring to the boil, then simmer gently for 15–18 minutes, stirring as often as possible, until the rice is tender and creamy. Stir in the grated courgette and defrosted peas for the final 2–3 minutes of cooking time.

- Season, then spoon the risotto into 4 warmed bowls. Scatter over the reserved golden bacon and shredded basil, if using. Serve with grated Parmesan cheese, if desired.

 Lazy Pea and Bacon Noodles

Heat 50 g (2 oz) butter in a large saucepan and cook 200 g (7 oz) finely chopped bacon over a medium-high heat, stirring occasionally, for 4–5 minutes until lightly golden. Pour over 600 ml (1 pint) boiling ham, chicken or vegetable stock, 2 tablespoons barbecue sauce, 200 g (7 oz) frozen peas and 400 g (13 oz) fresh noodles. Cover and simmer for 3–4 minutes until the peas and noodles are tender. Lift out the noodles and heap into bowls, then pour over the soup to serve.

 Lazy One-Pot Pea and Bacon Pasta

Melt 50 g (2 oz) butter in a large frying pan or saucepan and cook 250 g (8 oz) chopped bacon for 7–8 minutes until cooked and golden. Stir 300 g (10 oz) orzo (or use another small pasta shape, such as macaroni) into the pan, then add 500 ml (17 fl oz) hot chicken or vegetable stock. Bring to the boil, then reduce the heat and simmer gently for 8–10 minutes or until the pasta is just tender, adding a little more stock or boiling water if necessary. Stir 150 g (5 oz) frozen peas into the pan for the final 4–5 minutes of cooking. Spoon into 4 dishes and serve scattered with shredded basil and grated hard Italian cheese (such as Parmesan cheese), if desired.

10 Quick-Cook Pasta with Chillies and Anchovies

Serves 2

200 g (7 oz) quick-cook pasta
  (such as spaghetti or penne)
2 tablespoons olive oil
½–1 red chilli, deseeded and
  chopped
6 anchovies, drained and diced
1 tablespoons lemon juice
pepper

- Cook the pasta in a large pan of lightly salted boiling water for 3–5 minutes or according to the packet instructions until just tender. Drain the pasta, reserving 1 tablespoon of the cooking liquid.

- Toss with the remaining ingredients and reserved cooking liquid, then heap into warmed bowls to serve.

20 Wholewheat Spaghetti with Tomatoes and Anchovies

Bring a large pan of lightly salted water to the boil and cook 200 g (7 oz) wholewheat spaghetti for 11 minutes or according to the packet instructions until tender. Meanwhile, warm 3 tablespoons olive oil in a small pan and add 1 chopped garlic clove and 1 deseeded and chopped red chilli. Cook over a gentle heat for 2 minutes until just softened. Remove from the heat and set aside to allow the oil to infuse. Drain the pasta and return to the pan with 2 tablespoons cooking liquid. Toss immediately with the infused oil, 1 tablespoon lemon juice, 6 diced anchovies and 10 halved cherry tomatoes. Spoon into bowls and serve immediately.

30 Wholewheat Pasta Bake with Anchovies

Cook 200 g (7 oz) wholewheat pasta twists or penne in a pan of lightly salted boiling water for 11 minutes or according to the packet instructions until tender. Add 200 g (7 oz) broccoli florets for the final 2–3 minutes of cooking time. Meanwhile, heat 2 tablespoons oil in a frying pan and cook 1 finely chopped onion over a medium heat for 6–7 minutes until softened. Add 2 chopped garlic cloves and 1 finely chopped and deseeded red chilli and cook for a further 1–2 minutes until the onion, garlic and chilli are soft. Add a 450 g (14½ oz) jar of tomato-based pasta sauce and stir for a minute to heat. Drain the pasta and broccoli, then return to the pan and stir in the tomato sauce and 6 drained and chopped anchovy fillets. Season to taste, then tip into a small ovenproof dish and scatter over 75 g (3 oz) diced mozzarella or grated Cheddar cheese (or similar) and bake in a preheated oven, 200°C (400°F), Gas Mark 6, for about 15 minutes until bubbling and golden.

20 Tuna Gnocchi Bake

Serves 4

500 g (1 lb) potato gnocchi
2 x 400 g (13 oz) cans ratatouille
2 x 185 g (6½ oz) cans tuna in
    brine or oil, drained
125 g (4 oz) grated cheese (such
    as Cheddar cheese, Emmental
    or mozzarella)
crusty bread, to serve (optional)

- Bring a large pan of water to the boil and cook the gnocchi for 2–3 minutes or according to the packet instructions until they rise to the surface of the water. Drain well and return to the pan.

- Meanwhile, gently warm the ratatouille in a saucepan with the tuna, then pour over the gnocchi and stir gently to combine. Tip into a large, buttered ovenproof dish, then scatter with grated cheese and cook in a preheated oven, 220°C (425°F), Gas Mark 7, for about 15 minutes until bubbling and golden. Spoon into dishes and serve with crusty bread, if desired.

10 Cheesy Tuna Rarebit

Lightly toast 4 large or 8 small slices of brown bread. Meanwhile, beat 1 egg and add 200 g (7 oz) grated Cheddar or Lancashire cheese, 2 teaspoons Worcestershire sauce, 1 teaspoon mustard and 2–3 tablespoons milk or beer and mix well. Drain a 400 g (13 oz) can tuna and flake the fish over the toast. Spoon over the cheesy topping and cook under a grill preheated to a medium-hot setting for 3–4 minutes until the cheese is melted and golden. Serve with green salad, if desired.

30 Cheesy Tuna Puffs

In a bowl, mix the drained and flaked tuna from 2 x 185 g (6½ oz) cans, 2 chopped spring onions, 100 g (3½ oz) coarsely grated Cheddar cheese, 3 tablespoons mayonnaise, 1 tablespoon lemon juice and plenty of black pepper. Unroll a 375 g (12 oz) sheet of puff pastry and cut it into 8 equal-sized rectangles. Spoon the cheesy tuna over one half of a pastry rectangle, then brush the edges with a little beaten egg. Fold the other half over the filling, pressing down with your fingers. Using the back of a fork, press along the edges to seal the pastry attractively. Repeat to make 8 tuna puffs, then arrange these on a large baking sheet and bake in a preheated oven, 200°C (400°F), Gas Mark 6, for about 15 minutes until the pastry is puffed up and golden. Remove from the oven and serve with vegetables or a fresh green salad.

20 Lemon Butter Fried Fish

Serves 2

75 g (3 oz) butter
2 boneless chunky white fish
   fillets, about 175 g (6 oz) each
2 tablespoons chopped parsley
   or chives
1 teaspoon finely grated
   lemon rind
1 tablespoon lemon juice
salt and pepper

To serve

cooked rice or mashed potatoes
steamed spinach or broccoli
   (optional)

- Melt 25 g (1 oz) of the butter in a small non-stick frying pan. Lightly season the fish fillets with a pinch each of salt and pepper, then cook gently for 4–5 minutes on each side until golden and flaky. Remove the fish from the pan and set aside somewhere warm to rest.

- Meanwhile, add the remaining butter to the pan and heat gently until foamy. Stir in the herbs and lemon rind and juice, then remove from the heat.

- Arrange the fish fillets on plates with rice or mashed potatoes and steamed spinach or broccoli, if desired, and serve drizzled with the lemon butter.

---

10 Lemony Fish Pâté on Toast

Drain a 170 g (6 oz) can of herrings and place the fish in a bowl with 2 tablespoons cream cheese, 1 tablespoon lemon juice, a pinch of finely grated lemon rind, 1 tablespoon finely chopped chives and a generous pinch of black pepper. Mash with a fork until combined to a rough-textured pâté. Serve on crusty granary bread or oatcakes with watercress or baby spinach leaves and lemon wedges.

30 Lemony Baked Fish Parcels

Cut 2 large circles out of baking paper, and 2 more from a sheet of kitchen foil. Place 1 baking-paper layer on top of 1 foil layer, then repeat with the remaining circles. Arrange a generous handful of washed spinach leaves in the centre of each layered circle. Place a chunky white fish fillet that weighs about 175 g (6 oz) on top of each mound of spinach and top each with 25 g (1 oz) diced butter.

Scatter ½ teaspoon finely grated lemon rind, ½ tablespoon chopped parsley or chives and a pinch each of salt and pepper over each fillet and finish with a squeeze of lemon juice. Scrunch up the foil to seal the edges, then place on a baking sheet and bake in a preheated oven, 180°C (350°F), Gas Mark 4, for 15–20 minutes or until cooked and flaky. Serve the fish and spinach with new potatoes or rice and drizzled with the lemony butter juices.

STU-CHIL-DYP

10 Minted Potato, Red Onion and Feta Salad

Serves 2

567 g (1 lb 2½ oz) can new
  potatoes, drained
1 small bunch of mint, chopped
½ small red onion, finely sliced
1 tablespoon lemon juice
100 g (3½ oz) feta cheese, diced
  or crumbled

- Place the new potatoes in a large bowl with the mint, red onion and lemon juice and toss gently to combine.

- Divide the salad between 2 dishes. Scatter over the feta cheese and serve.

20 Minty Pea, Red Onion and Feta Omelette with Salad

Heat 1 tablespoon olive or vegetable oil in a frying pan and cook 1 small thinly sliced red onion over a medium heat for 6–7 minutes until softened. Meanwhile, cook 150 g (5 oz) frozen peas in a pan of boiling water for 3–4 minutes until just tender, then drain and add to the pan of onions with 200 g (7 oz) sliced cooked new potatoes, 4 lightly beaten eggs, 1 tablespoon chopped mint and a pinch each of salt and pepper. Cook gently, without stirring, for 4–5 minutes until almost set, then scatter over 100 g (3½ oz) crumbled feta and cook under a grill preheated to a medium-high setting for 3–5 minutes until set and golden. Slice into wedges and serve with salad leaves.

30 Mint, Red Onion and Feta Rice Salad

Cook 200 g (7 oz) long-grain and wild rice mix in a large pan of lightly salted boiling water for 20–25 minutes until just tender. Cool under running cold water, then drain well. Meanwhile, combine the finely grated rind and juice of 1 lime in a large bowl with 2 tablespoons olive or vegetable oil, half a finely chopped red onion, 1 small bunch of chopped mint and 50 g (2 oz) roughly chopped pitted black olives (optional). Stir this mixture through the rice with 50 g (2 oz) crumbled feta and ¼ cucumber, deseeded and diced, then spoon the salad into 2 dishes and serve scattered with an extra 50 g (2 oz) diced or crumbled feta cheese and lime wedges, if desired.

30 Stove-Top Chorizo Pizza

Serves 2

145 g (5 oz) pizza base mix
100 ml (3½ fl oz) lukewarm water
1½ tablespoons tomato purée
2 teaspoons tomato ketchup
2 teaspoons olive or vegetable oil
pinch of dried oregano
50 g (2 oz) thinly sliced chorizo
   sausage
125 g (4 oz) mozzarella, sliced
salt and pepper
2 small handfuls of rocket leaves,
   to serve

- Make up the pizza base mix by mixing with the lukewarm water and knead for 4–5 minutes or until smooth. (Alternatively, follow the packet instructions.) Roll out the dough to make a 30 cm (12 inch) circle and set aside to rest for 8 minutes.

- Heat a large dry frying pan until hot and carefully lower the pizza base inside. Cook over a medium heat for about 10 minutes, turning once, until lightly golden.

- Meanwhile, make the pizza sauce. Mix the tomato purée, ketchup, oil, oregano and a pinch each of salt and pepper. Spread thinly over the pizza base in the pan and scatter over the chorizo and mozzarella. Continue to cook for a further 2–3 minutes, then place under a grill preheated to a medium-hot setting for 1–2 minutes until melting and bubbling. (If you do not have a grill, cook the pizza base for 4–5 minutes until 1 side is golden. Flip over, top with the sauce and toppings, then cook for a further 6–7 minutes until the base is golden and the cheese is melting.)

- Cut into slices and serve topped with the rocket leaves.

 ### 10 Under-the-Grill Chorizo Pizza

Make up the pizza sauce as above and spread very thinly over 2 large plain tortilla wraps or square wraps. Scatter over the toppings as above, then drizzle with a teaspoon olive oil and place under a grill preheated to a medium-hot setting for 4–5 minutes until crisp and melting. Serve in wedges with lots of rocket salad.

 ### 20 Oven-Baked Chorizo Pizza

Make up the pizza sauce as above and spread over 2 ready-made mini pizza bases. Top with 50 g (2 oz) thinly sliced chorizo sausage and 125 g (4 oz) sliced mozzarella. Scatter 1 small handful of rocket over each one, then drizzle with a teaspoon olive oil and bake in a preheated oven, 220°C (425°F), Gas Mark 7, for 8–10 minutes or according to the packet instructions until melted and lightly golden. Serve with extra rocket salad.

 # Jalepeño Turkey Burgers

Serves 4

500 g (1 lb) fresh turkey mince
1 tablespoon finely chopped
  jalepeño pepper
2 tablespoons finely chopped
  coriander (optional)
3 spring onions, finely chopped
1 small egg, lightly beaten
2 tablespoons vegetable oil
salt and pepper

To serve

ciabatta-style rolls or crusty rolls
shredded Iceberg lettuce
  (optional)
spicy salsa (optional)
soured cream (optional)

- Place the minced turkey in a bowl with the jalepeño pepper, coriander (if using), spring onion and egg, then season with a pinch each of salt and pepper. Mix well to combine, then shape into 4 patties.

- Heat the oil in a large non-stick frying pan over a medium heat and shallow-fry the burgers gently for 4–5 minutes on each side or until cooked through and golden.

- Arrange the burgers on the bread rolls with your desired fillings. Top with the lid and serve immediately.

---

10 Jalepeño Turkey Melt

Cut open 4 large bread rolls or ciabatta-style rolls and spread the cut sides with 150 g (5 oz) spicy salsa (optional). Layer 75 g (3 oz) wafer-thin sliced turkey over each open roll. Scatter 1 teaspoon sliced jalepeño peppers, half a sliced tomato and half a thinly sliced spring onion over each sandwich and top each with 2 cheese slices. Arrange on a baking sheet and cook under a grill preheated to a medium setting for 2–3 minutes until the cheese is melted and bubbling. Serve hot with shredded Iceberg lettuce.

30 Jalepeño Turkey Chilli

Heat 2 tablespoons vegetable oil in a large frying pan or saucepan and cook 1 chopped onion and 1 chopped red pepper for 6–7 minutes until slightly softened. Stir in 400 g (13 oz) sliced turkey breast meat and cook for 2–3 minutes, stirring frequently, until lightly browned all over. Stir in a 41 g (1½ oz) packet of chilli con carne spice mix, 400 g (13 oz) can chopped tomatoes, 400 g (13 oz) can kidney beans, rinsed and drained, and 100 ml (3½ fl oz) lager or water. Stir to combine, season lightly, then cover and simmer gently for about 15 minutes until rich and thick, stirring occasionally and adding more liquid if needed. Scatter over 2 tablespoons chopped jalepeño peppers and serve heaped onto cooked rice with chopped coriander, if desired.

10 Veggie Noodle Salad

Serves 2

100 g (3½ oz) rice or thread
   noodles
75 g (3 oz) bean sprouts
75 g (3 oz) baby spinach leaves
   or shredded Iceberg lettuce
1 carrot, peeled and grated
½ small red onion, thinly sliced,
   or 2 spring onions, sliced
1 tablespoon crushed toasted
   peanuts, to serve (optional)

Dressing

1 tablespoon vegetable oil
1 tablespoon soy sauce
2 tablespoons lime juice

- Place the noodles in a large bowl with enough boiling water to cover them. Set aside for 3–4 minutes or according to the packet instructions until just tender. Drain through a sieve and rinse under cold water to cool. Return the rinsed and drained noodles to the bowl.

- While the noodles are cooking, combine the ingredients for the dressing.

- Pour the dressing over the noodles. Add the vegetables and toss gently to combine. Heap into bowls and serve immediately, topped with crushed peanuts, if desired.

20 Bowl of Veggie Noodles

Heat 2 tablespoons vegetable oil in a wok and add 1 sliced onion and 1 sliced red pepper. Stir-fry for 2–3 minutes until they begin to soften. Cut 1 small peeled carrot into thin sticks, add to the pan and stir-fry for 2–3 minutes. Stir in 100 g (3½ oz) bean sprouts and cook for 1 minute, then add 300 g (10 oz) cooked medium egg noodles and toss for 1–2 minutes or according to the packet instructions until hot. Mix in 200 g (7 oz) of your preferred stir-fry sauce. Heap into 2 warmed bowls and serve immediately, scattered with 1 tablespoon crushed cashew nuts.

30 Veggie Soupy Noodles

Heat 2 tablespoons vegetable oil in a saucepan or wok and cook 1 sliced onion and 1 sliced red pepper over a medium heat for 7–8 minutes until softened. Add 150 g (5 oz) sliced mushrooms and 2 sliced garlic cloves and cook for a further 3–4 minutes until tender. Pour in 500 ml (17 fl oz) hot vegetable stock, 2 tablespoons soy sauce and 1 star anise (optional). Bring to the boil, reduce the heat and simmer, covered, for 4–5 minutes to allow the flavours to develop. Add 150 g (5 oz) dried medium egg noodles to the pan, then remove from the heat and set aside for 4–5 minutes or until the noodles are just tender. Heap the noodles into 2 deep bowls or dishes, then remove and discard the star anise and pour the soupy vegetables over the noodles. Scatter with roughly chopped coriander to serve, if desired.

10 Chilli Pea Pasta

Serves 2

3 tablespoons olive oil
½–1 red chilli, deseeded and
  finely sliced
2 garlic cloves, chopped
200 g (7 oz) frozen peas
400 g (13 oz) quick-cook pasta
  (such as penne or fusilli)
grated Parmesan cheese or other
  hard Italian cheese, to serve
  (optional)

- Heat the olive oil in a small pan and cook the chilli and garlic over a low heat for 2 minutes until softened but not coloured. Set aside to infuse.

- Bring a large pan of lightly salted water to the boil and cook the pasta and peas for 3–5 minutes or according to the packet instructions until both are just tender. Drain and return to the pan, reserving 2 tablespoons of the cooking liquid.

- Stir the infused oil into the pasta and peas with the reserved cooking liquid and spoon into 2 warmed bowls to serve, sprinkled with grated cheese, if desired.

 Chilli Pea Soup Heat 2 tablespoons vegetable oil in a pan and cook 1 large finely chopped onion over a medium heat for 6–7 minutes. Add ½–1 chopped red chilli, 1 tablespoon korma curry paste and 1 chopped garlic clove and cook for a further 2–3 minutes. Pour in 600 ml (1 pint) hot vegetable stock and boil. Tip in 400 g (13 oz) frozen peas, then simmer gently for 3–4 minutes until tender. Take off the heat and blend using a hand-held or jug blender (or stir in 200 g/7 oz leftover couscous or rice with the peas and eat as a soupy stew). Season and serve drizzled with chilli oil.

 Chilli Pea and Pulse Korma Rinse 100 g (3½ oz) dried red lentils in plenty of water and cook in a pan of lightly salted boiling water for 15–20 minutes until the lentils are almost tender but are still holding their shape, then drain. Meanwhile, heat 2 tablespoons vegetable oil in a large frying pan or saucepan and cook 1 large finely chopped onion over a medium heat for 7–8 minutes, to soften. Add 1 thinly sliced garlic clove and 1 deseeded and chopped green chilli and cook for a further 2 minutes until the onion, garlic and chilli are softened but not coloured. Stir in 3 tablespoons korma paste and cook for 1 minute. Stir in 125 ml (4 fl oz) water and 100 ml (3½ fl oz) double cream and bring to the boil. Stir in 100 g (3½ oz) frozen garden peas and a 210 g (7⅓ oz) can chickpeas, rinsed and drained, and simmer gently for 4–5 minutes until the peas are tender. Stir in the drained lentils and simmer for a further 2–3 minutes until the korma is rich and thick. Serve in bowls with naan bread and poppadoms, if desired.

STU-CHIL-LYX

30 Sweet and Sour Pork

Serves 4

3 tablespoons vegetable oil
350 g (11½ oz) cubed pork
1 large onion, cut into bite-sized pieces
1 red or yellow pepper, cut into bite-sized pieces
150 g (5 oz) tomato ketchup (about 8 tablespoons)
3 tablespoons dark soft brown sugar
225 g (7½ oz) can pineapple chunks in juice
3 tablespoons malt vinegar
1 tablespoon light soy sauce
cooked rice, to serve

- Heat the oil in a large frying pan and fry the pork over a medium-high heat for 5–6 minutes until golden brown all over. Add the onion and pepper and cook for a further 6–7 minutes until the vegetables are beginning to soften. Add the ketchup, sugar, pineapple and its juice, vinegar and soy sauce and bring to the boil, stirring frequently.

- Reduce the heat and simmer gently for about 10–12 minutes until the sauce is thick and the pork is thoroughly cooked. Serve with cooked rice.

10 Sweet and Sour Pork Noodles

Cook 375 g (12 oz) medium egg noodles in a pan of boiling water for 4 minutes, then drain. Meanwhile, heat 2 tablespoons oil in a wok and cook 350 g (11½ oz) pork stir-fry strips for 2 minutes over a high heat. Add 4 spring onions cut into 2.5 cm (1 inch) lengths with 100 g (3½ oz) shredded mangetout or thinly sliced baby corn. Stir-fry for 2 minutes. Add a 440 g (14½ oz) jar of sweet and sour sauce. Simmer gently, stirring frequently, for 3–4 minutes until the pork is cooked thoroughly, then toss through the noodles and serve.

20 Sweet Chilli Pork Stir-Fry

Heat 3 tablespoons vegetable oil in a large frying pan or wok and cook 2 chopped garlic cloves and 1 tablespoon peeled and chopped fresh root ginger (optional) for 1–2 minutes until softened. Add 350 g (11½ oz) minced pork to the pan for 6–7 minutes, stirring frequently, until the meat is browned. Add a 200 g (7 oz) mixture of halved baby corn and halved mangetout and stir-fry for a further 2–3 minutes until slightly softened. Stir 5 tablespoons sweet chilli sauce and about 2 tablespoons light soy sauce into the pan with 450 g (14½ oz) cooked ready-to-eat udon or thick rice noodles. Stir for 2–3 minutes until hot, then heap into bowls to serve.

STU-CHIL-VYZ

10 Spaghetti with Garlic and Black Pepper

Serves 2

200 g (7 oz) quick-cook
   spaghetti
3 tablespoons olive oil
2 garlic cloves, chopped
2 tablespoons lemon juice
pepper
grated Parmesan cheese,
   to serve

- Cook the spaghetti in a large pan of lightly salted water for 3–5 minutes or according to the packet instructions until just tender. Drain and return to the pan, reserving 3 tablespoons of the cooking water.

- Meanwhile, heat the oil in a frying pan with the garlic and warm gently for 2–3 minutes until softened but not coloured. Pour over the cooked spaghetti with the reserved cooking liquid and lemon juice. Season with pepper. Heap into warmed bowls and serve with grated Parmesan.

---

20 Garlicky Spaghetti Carbonara

Cook 200 g (7 oz) spaghetti in a pan of lightly salted boiling water for 10–12 minutes until tender. Meanwhile, heat 2 tablespoons oil in a frying pan and cook 150 g (5 oz) chopped bacon for 4–5 minutes over a medium heat. Add 2 chopped garlic cloves and cook for 1 minute. Set aside. Beat 1 large egg and 1 egg yolk with 4 tablespoons single or double cream, black pepper and 3 tablespoons grated hard Italian cheese. Drain the pasta and return to the pan with the bacon and the cream. Stir for a minute over a very low heat to heat and coat in the sauce. Serve with extra cheese.

---

30 Garlicky Macaroni Cheese

Cook 200 g (7 oz) macaroni in a large pan of lightly salted boiling water for 8–10 minutes until tender. Meanwhile, place 25 g (1 oz) plain flour, 25 g (1 oz) butter and 250 ml (8 fl oz) milk in a saucepan and heat gently, stirring constantly, until thickened. Simmer gently for 2 minutes, then remove from the heat and stir in 75 g (3 oz) grated medium or mature Cheddar cheese. Heat 2 tablespoons olive or vegetable oil in a frying pan and cook 200 g (7 oz) chopped bacon for 4–5 minutes over a medium heat. Add 2 chopped garlic cloves and cook for 1 minute. Stir the garlicky bacon into the cheese sauce. Drain the pasta and stir it into the garlicky cheese sauce. Tip the whole lot into an ovenproof dish, sprinkle with 75 g (3 oz) grated medium or mature Cheddar cheese and bake in a preheated oven, 220°C (425°F), Gas Mark 7, for about 15 minutes until bubbling and golden (or cook under a grill preheated to a medium setting for 3–4 minutes until the cheese is melted and golden, or just spoon into bowls and serve with extra grated cheese). Serve with salad.

STU-CHIL-KEH

30 Chorizo and Bean Stew

Serves 4

2 tablespoons olive or
   vegetable oil
225 g (7½ oz) chorizo sausage,
   diced
1 onion, thickly sliced
1 red pepper, thickly sliced
2 garlic cloves, chopped or
   sliced (optional)
2 x 400 g (13 oz) cans chopped
   tomatoes
1 teaspoon dried oregano or
   mixed herbs (optional)
2 x 400 g (13 oz) cans beans
   (such as butter beans or
   cannellini beans), drained
2 tablespoons chopped parsley
   (optional)
salt and pepper

- Heat the oil in a large saucepan or frying pan and cook the chorizo, onion, pepper and garlic for about 10 minutes until the vegetables are softened.
- Add the tomatoes, herbs and beans, then cover and simmer gently for 15–18 minutes until the stew is rich and thick.
- Season to taste, then ladle into bowls and serve scattered with chopped parsley, if desired.

---

10 Chorizo'd Bowl of Baked Beans

Heat 2 tablespoons olive or vegetable oil in a large saucepan and add 1 finely chopped onion. Cook over a medium heat for 7–8 minutes to soften. Add 100 g (3½ oz) shredded sliced chorizo sausage to the onions for the final minute of cooking. Add 2 x 400 g (13 oz) cans baked beans in tomato sauce and stir for a further 1–2 minutes until hot. Serve immediately, spooned over slices of hot buttered toast.

20 Chorizo and Beans with Penne

Heat 2 tablespoons olive or vegetable oil and cook 1 finely chopped red onion and 200 g (7 oz) diced chorizo sausage over a medium heat for 7–8 minutes until the onion has softened. Add 2 chopped garlic cloves for the final 2 minutes of cooking. Pour 500 g (1 lb) sieved tomatoes or passata into the pan with 1 teaspoon dried oregano and a pinch each of sugar, salt and pepper. Cover and simmer gently for about 10 minutes until thickened slightly. Stir in a 300 g (10 oz) can broad beans or 400 g (13 oz) butter beans, rinsed and drained, for the final 3–4 minutes of cooking time. Meanwhile, cook 400 g (13 oz) penne pasta in a large pan of salted boiling water for 10–12 minutes or according to the packet instructions until just tender. Drain and serve heaped into 4 warm bowls, topped with the chorizo sauce.

STU-CHIL-HUX

Beef and Onion Wraps

Serves 4

2 tablespoons vegetable oil
350 g (11½ oz) beef stir-fry strips
1 red onion, thinly sliced
1 red pepper, thinly sliced
30 g (1¼ oz) Mexican spice mix
  (such as fajita seasoning)
4 large or 8 small soft flour
  tortillas

For the filling (optional)

salsa
grated Cheddar cheese or
  Emmental
shredded Iceberg lettuce

- Heat the oil in a large frying pan and cook the beef over a high heat for 2–3 minutes until browned. Add the onion and peppers and stir-fry for 2–3 minutes until the vegetables begin to soften and the beef is just cooked but still slightly pink. Sprinkle over the Mexican spice mix and stir-fry for a minute to cook the spices.

- Divide the beef between the tortillas and top with your chosen fillings, then roll each tortilla tightly and cut it in half diagonally to serve.

Beef and Crispy Onion Burgers

Heat 2 tablespoons oil in a frying pan and add 2 sliced onions. Cook over a medium heat for 15–18 minutes, turning occasionally, until crisp and golden. Drain on kitchen paper. Meanwhile, put 500 g (1 lb) minced beef in a bowl with 1 teaspoon dried oregano, 1 crushed garlic clove and seasoning. Add 1 small beaten egg and mix with your hands to form 4 patties. Heat 2 tablespoons oil in a frying pan and cook for 3–5 minutes on each side. Serve on burger buns with crispy onions and garnishes (such Cheddar cheese or pickle slices, shredded Iceburg lettuce, spicy salsa or American mustard).

Beef and Onion Stew

Heat 2 tablespoons olive or vegetable oil in a large non-stick frying pan and cook 350 g (11½ oz) beef stir-fry strips over a medium-high heat for 2–3 minutes until browned. Remove with a slotted spoon and set aside. Reduce the heat slightly and add 1 large sliced onion and 2 chopped garlic cloves to the pan for 6–7 minutes until softened and lightly coloured. Stir in 1 tablespoon plain flour and 1 tablespoon paprika for 1 minute, then add a 400 g (13 oz) can chopped tomatoes, 1 tablespoon tomato purée and 300 ml (½ pint) hot beef or vegetable stock. Bring to the boil and simmer gently for 15–17 minutes until rich and thick. Return the beef to the pan with any juices and stir to heat. Stir in 4 tablespoons single cream and serve with cooked rice and chopped parsley to garnish, if desired.

QuickCook
Supper for Friends

Recipes listed by cooking time

30

Teriyaki Baked Salmon 180

Tomato and Basil Soup 182

Mexican Chilli
Beef Burger 184

Spiced Lamb Kebab
with Couscous 186

Thai Fishcakes
with Dipping Sauce 188

Green Pepper and
Mushroom Stroganoff 190

Bacon-Wrapped
Pesto Chicken 192

Apple and Brie-Stuffed
Pork 194

Poor Man's Pesto
Pasta Bake 196

Smoked Ham, Chicken
and Cheese Puff Parcels 198

Classic Cheese Fondue 200

Lemony Spinach and
Mackerel Bake 202

Turkey Tikka Masala 204

Margherita Tart 206

Sticky Barbecue Pork
with Wedges 208

Aromatic Prawn Pilau 210

One-Pan Sausage Roast 212

Creamy Mushroom
and Chive Risotto 214

Herby Crust Fish
with Mash 216

Sweet Potato and
Green Bean Curry 218

Roasted Peppers
with Mozzarella
and Couscous 220

Ginger Marinated Tofu
and Vegetable Parcels 222

Vegetable Curry
with Rice 224

Fisherman's Pie
with Sardines 226

2

Teriyaki Salmon Skewers 180

Tomato and Basil
Spaghetti 182

Mexican Beef Fajitas 184

Spiced Lamb Burgers
with Couscous 186

Thai Red Fish Curry 188

Mushroom and Mixed
Pepper Fold-Over 190

Wholewheat Pesto
Spaghetti with Bacon 192

Grilled Gammon
with Apple and Brie 194

Poor Man's Pesto
with Penne 196

Smoked Bacon and
Chicken Parcels 198

Creamy Blue Cheese
Fondue 200

Lemony Mackerel
Spaghetti 202

Turkey Tikka Skewers 204

Margherita Pizza 206

Barbecue Pork Steaks
with Corn and Rice 208

Creamy Curried Prawns 210

One-Pan Sausage
Casserole 212

10

Creamy Mushroom
and Chive Linguine 214

Breaded Fish with
Mushy Peas 216

Green Vegetable Curry 218

Grilled Pepper and
Cheese Couscous 220

Gingery Tofu Stir-Fry 222

Curried Vegetable
and Rice Bowl 224

Fisherman's Sardine
Linguine 226

Teriyaki Salmon Noodles 180

Tomato and Basil
Bruschetta 182

Mexican Bean Tostada 184

Spiced Lambs' Liver
with Couscous 186

Thai Prawn Curry 188

Baguette Pizza with
Mushrooms and Peppers 190

Crispy Bacon and
Pesto Pasta Salad 192

Apple, Brie and Ham
Melts 194

Poor Man's Pesto
Pasta Salad 196

Chicken, Ham and
Cheese Parcels 198

Quick Cheat's Fondue 200

Flaked Mackerel Salad
with Lemon Dressing 202

Tandoori Turkey Steaks
with Rice 204

Margherita Salad 206

Chinese-Style Barbecue
Pork Pot Noodles 208

Coronation Prawn Wraps 210

One-Pan Sausage
Omelette 212

Grilled Mushrooms with
Polenta and Chives 214

Grilled Fish Fingers
with Peas 216

Green Curry Noodle Soup 218

Quick Pepper and
Mozzarella Salad 220

Gingery Grilled Tofu
with Noodles 222

Vegetable Rice with
Curry Sauce 224

Fisherman's Sardine
and Potato Salad 226

1 Teriyaki Salmon Noodles

Serves 4

375 g (12 oz) medium egg noodles
3 tablespoons vegetable oil
3 spring onions, thickly sliced,
  plus 1 extra, finely sliced, to
  garnish (optional)
2.5 cm (1 inch) piece of fresh
  root ginger, peeled and cut
  into thin matchsticks
250 g (8 oz) teriyaki stir-fry sauce
2 x 180 g (6¼ oz) cans skinless,
  boneless salmon, drained
  and flaked

- Cook the noodles in a pan of boiling water for 3–4 minutes or according to the packet instructions until just tender. Drain and toss in 1 tablespoon oil to prevent sticking.

- Meanwhile, heat the remaining oil in a large frying pan set over a medium heat and cook the spring onion and ginger for 2–3 minutes until softened and lightly coloured. Stir the noodles and the teriyaki sauce into the pan and toss together to coat.

- Flake over the salmon and heat gently for 1–2 minutes until hot. Heap into dishes to serve, garnished with some very finely sliced spring onion, if desired.

 Teriyaki Salmon Skewers

Place 400 g (13 oz) chunky cubed salmon fillet in a bowl and pour over 4 tablespoons teriyaki sauce. Mix to thoroughly coat the fish, then marinate in the refrigerator for 5–10 minutes. Thread onto 4 large or 8 small metal skewers. Cook under a grill preheated to a medium setting for about 8 minutes, turning occasionally, until just cooked through. Serve the skewers on a bed of rice or noodles and stir-fried vegetables, if desired.

 Teriyaki Baked Salmon

Arrange 4 skinless, boneless chunky salmon fillets in a shallow ovenproof dish and drizzle 1 tablespoon teriyaki marinade over each one. Rub the marinade into the fillets and marinate in the refrigerator for 10 minutes. Cook in a preheated oven, 190°C (375°F), Gas Mark 5, for 12–15 minutes until just cooked but slightly pink in the centre. Set aside to rest for 2–3 minutes. Meanwhile, cook the noodles as above, as well as the spring onion and ginger. Toss the noodles with the cooked spring onion and ginger until hot, then heap into warmed dishes and serve topped with the salmon and any juices.

30 Tomato and Basil Soup

Serves 4

2 tablespoons olive or
  vegetable oil
1 large onion, chopped
2 garlic cloves, chopped
500 g (1 lb) passata or sieved
  Italian tomatoes
400 g (13 oz) can chickpeas,
  rinsed and drained
500 ml (17 fl oz) hot vegetable
  or chicken stock
1 small bunch of basil, roughly
  chopped
salt and pepper

- Heat the oil in a large saucepan and cook the onion over a medium heat for 7–8 minutes until softened. Add the garlic and cook gently for a further 2 minutes until softened.

- Pour the passata and chickpeas into the pan with the hot stock, then bring to the boil and simmer gently for 15 minutes until rich and thickened slightly.

- Add the basil leaves, reserving a few for garnish. Season to taste, then blend with a hand-held blender until smooth and thick, adding a little extra water for the desired consistency. (Don't worry if you do not have a blender; this soup can be served as a chunky version.)

- Ladle into warmed mugs to serve and garnish with the reserved basil leaves.

1 Tomato and Basil Bruschetta

Dice 8 tomatoes and tip into a bowl with 1 small bunch of chopped basil, ½ finely chopped red onion, 2 tablespoons olive oil and 2 teaspoons red wine vinegar. Season well and stir gently to combine. Toast 8 slices of rustic-style bread, then rub one side of each slice with a halved garlic clove. Arrange the toasts on serving plates with rocket leaves, if desired, and spoon over the tomato-and-basil topping. Serve immediately.

2 Tomato and Basil Spaghetti

Heat 2 tablespoons vegetable oil in a large saucepan and cook 1 finely chopped onion over a medium heat for 7–8 minutes until softened. Pour 500 g (1 lb) basil or plain passata into the pan with a pinch each of sugar, salt and pepper and bring to the boil. Reduce the heat and simmer gently for 8–10 minutes until thickened. Meanwhile, cook 400 g (13 oz) spaghetti in a large pan of lightly salted boiling water for 11 minutes or according to the packet instructions until just tender. Drain and stir into the tomato sauce with 1 small bunch of roughly chopped basil leaves. Heap into 4 warmed bowls and serve with grated cheese.

STU-SUPP-RUB

30 Mexican Chilli Beef Burger

Serves 4

3 tablespoons vegetable oil
1 onion, finely chopped
1 red pepper, finely chopped
40 g (1½ oz) Mexican spice mix
  (such as fajita seasoning)
1 teaspoon dried oregano
400 g (13 oz) minced beef

To serve

soft tortilla wraps or toasted
  burger buns
grated Cheddar cheese (optional)
spicy salsa (optional)
Iceberg lettuce (optional)

- Heat 2 tablespoons of the oil in a frying pan and cook the onion and red pepper over a medium heat for 10 minutes until really soft and golden. Scrape into a large bowl and set aside to cool for 2–3 minutes before adding the remaining ingredients. Mix really well with your hands, then shape into 4 patties.

- Return the pan to the heat with the remaining oil and cook the burgers over a medium heat for 4–5 minutes on each side until cooked but still juicy.

- Serve the chilli beef burgers in folded tortillas or toasted burger buns with fillings such as grated Cheddar cheese, salsa and shredded Iceberg lettuce, if desired.

1 Mexican Bean Tostada

Heat a frying pan and lightly toast a large soft tortilla wrap for 1 minute on each side. Push into a deep bowl and repeat with 3 more tortillas. Meanwhile, mix a 400 g (13 oz) can red kidney beans, rinsed and drained, with 1 small finely chopped red onion, 1 finely chopped red or yellow pepper, 1 peeled, stoned and diced avocado and 1 small bunch chopped coriander. Drizzle over 2 tablespoons oil and 1 tablespoon lime juice. Season to taste. Drop some shredded Iceberg lettuce into each tortilla and divide the beans between them. Serve with grated Cheddar cheese, spicy salsa and soured cream.

2 Mexican Beef Fajitas

Stir a 40 g (1½ oz) packet fajita seasoning into 350 g (11½ oz) beef stir-fry strips and set aside. Heat 2 tablespoons vegetable oil in a large frying pan and cook 1 sliced onion and 1 sliced red pepper over a high heat for 3–4 minutes, stirring occasionally, until lightly charred and slightly softened. Tip into a bowl and return the pan to the heat with a further 2 tablespoons oil. Add the beef stir-fry strips and cook for 3–4 minutes, turning occasionally, until they are just cooked and browned all over. Return the vegetables to the pan for a minute until really hot and sizzling. Serve the sizzling

Mexican beef with warmed soft tortilla wraps and a choice of extra fillings (such as grated Cheddar cheese, shredded Iceberg lettuce, jalapeño slices, spicy salsa and soured cream).

30 Spiced Lamb Kebab with Couscous

Serves 4

300 g (10 oz) diced lamb

2 garlic cloves, crushed

1 teaspoon ground cumin

1 teaspoon ground coriander

2 tablespoons finely chopped mint

2 tablespoons olive or
  vegetable oil

1 large onion, cut into bite-sized
  pieces

1 large green pepper, cut into
  bite-sized pieces

2 tomatoes, each cut into
  6 wedges

To serve

steamed couscous

garlic sauce or tzatziki

- Place the lamb in a bowl with the garlic, spices, mint and 1 tablespoon of the oil, then rub really well to coat the meat in the spices. Marinate in the refrigerator for at least 15 minutes.

- Thread the lamb onto 4 long metal skewers, alternating with the onion, green pepper and tomato wedges. Arrange on the rack of a foil-lined grill tray, drizzle with the remaining oil and cook under a hot grill for 7–10 minutes, turning occasionally, until everything is lightly charred and the lamb is cooked to your liking.

- Serve the kebab skewers with bowls of steamed couscous, and garlic sauce or tzatziki, if desired.

---

1 Spiced Lambs' Liver with Couscous

In a bowl, mix 350 g (11½ oz) lambs' liver with 1 teaspoon each of ground cumin and coriander, ¼ teaspoon ground cinnamon, ½ teaspoon ground black pepper and ¼ teaspoon ground cayenne pepper. Drizzle over 1 tablespoon olive or vegetable oil and mix really well to combine. Heat 1 tablespoon oil in a large non-stick frying pan and cook the lambs' liver for 3–4 minutes until browned all over and just cooked through, but still juicy.

Spoon the spiced livers over bowls of steamed couscous with shredded Iceberg lettuce or red cabbage and a dollop of garlic sauce and drizzle with any juices.

2 Spiced Lamb Burgers with Couscous

Place 400 g (13 oz) minced lamb in a bowl with 1 teaspoon each of ground cumin and coriander, ¼ teaspoon ground cinnamon, ½ teaspoon dried mint, 1 teaspoon onion granules and 2 crushed garlic cloves. Mix well, then shape into 4 patties. Heat 2 tablespoons oil in a frying pan and cook the burgers for 4–5 minutes on each side until cooked through, but juicy. Serve with couscous and coleslaw.

STU-SUPP-ZOH

30 Thai Fishcakes with Dipping Sauce

Serves 4

500 g (1 lb) boneless fish fillets
(such as salmon, cod or pollack),
cut into chunks

1–2 tablespoons Thai red
curry paste

1 tablespoon fish sauce or
lime juice

1 small bunch of coriander,
finely chopped

2 spring onions, finely sliced

1 small egg white, whisked

4 tablespoons vegetable oil

sweet chilli sauce, to serve

- Place the fish in a food processor and pulse until it forms a chunky paste. Scrape into a bowl and mix with the curry paste, fish sauce or lime juice, coriander, spring onion and egg white until well combined. Use slightly wet hands to form the mixture into about 16 little fishcakes. Arrange on a large plate, cover with clingfilm and chill in the refrigerator for about 20 minutes. (Alternatively, if you do not own a food processor, chop the fish as finely as possible and mix with the remaining ingredients, then form into 4 large patties. Chill for 15 minutes.)

- Heat the oil in a large frying pan and cook the fishcakes for about 2 minutes on each side (or 3–4 minutes on each side, if cooking 4 larger patties) until cooked through and golden. Drain on kitchen paper and serve with the sweet chilli dipping sauce.

1 **Thai Prawn Curry**
Heat 2 tablespoons oil in a frying pan and cook 3 sliced spring onions with 2 chopped garlic cloves for 2–3 minutes. Stir in a 500 g (1 lb) jar of Thai-style coconut curry sauce and boil. Add 400 g (13 oz) raw peeled prawns, then simmer gently for 2–3 minutes or until cooked and pink. Serve spooned over bowls of cooked rice, garnished with chopped coriander.

2 **Thai Red Fish Curry**
Heat 2 tablespoons vegetable oil in a frying pan or saucepan and add 1 tablespoon Thai red curry paste. Stir over a gentle heat for 1 minute to cook the spices, then pour in a 400 ml (14 fl oz) can coconut milk and 300 ml (½ pint) hot chicken or vegetable stock and bring to the boil. Simmer gently for 8–10 minutes to allow the flavours to develop, then stir in 400 g (13 oz) bite-sized chunks of white fish (such as pollack or coley). Simmer gently for 3–4 minutes until the fish is just cooked, then stir through 1 tablespoon fish sauce or lime juice (optional). Spoon the mixture over bowls of rice and garnish with freshly chopped coriander, to serve.

STU-SUPP-CUL

30 Green Pepper and Mushroom Stroganoff

Serves 4

50 g (2 oz) butter
2 tablespoons olive or
   vegetable oil
1 onion, halved and sliced
1 large green pepper, sliced
500 g (1 lb) mushrooms,
   thickly sliced or halved
   (depending on size)
2 teaspoons paprika
1 tablespoons plain flour
300 ml (½ pint) hot vegetable
   stock
150 ml (5 fl oz) soured cream
   (or use double cream mixed
   with 2 teaspoons lemon juice)
2 tablespoons chopped parsley
salt and pepper
cooked tagliatelle or rice, to serve

- Melt the butter with the oil in a large frying pan and cook the onion and pepper over a medium heat for 7–8 minutes. Add the mushrooms and cook for 5–6 minutes, stirring occasionally, until golden and softened, then stir in the paprika and flour for 1 minute.

- Stir the vegetable stock into the pan and bring to the boil. Reduce the heat, season with salt and pepper to taste and simmer gently for 8–10 minutes until thickened slightly.

- Remove from the heat and stir in the soured cream and chopped parsley. Serve immediately, spooned over cooked tagliatelle or rice.

 Baguette Pizza with Mushrooms and Peppers Cut 1 small French stick in half and split each half horizontally. Arrange, cut side up, on a baking sheet and spread each with 2 tablespoons pizza topping sauce. Divide 150 g (5 oz) finely sliced mushrooms and 1 finely sliced green or red pepper between the pizza bases, then top each one with a small handful of grated cheese (such as Cheddar cheese or mozzarella). Cook under a grill preheated to a medium setting for 3–4 minutes. Serve hot with green salad.

 Mushroom and Mixed Pepper Fold-Over Spread 2 tablespoons pizza topping sauce over 1 large soft tortilla wrap and repeat with 3 more tortillas. Scatter over 1 finely sliced red pepper and 1 finely sliced green pepper, 150 g (5 oz) finely sliced mushrooms, a 125 g (4 oz) ball of mozzarella, diced, and 125 g (4 oz) coarsely grated Cheddar cheese. Fold each tortilla in half to envelope the filling. Heat 1 teaspoon olive or vegetable oil in a large frying pan and cook 2 of the fold-overs for about 5 minutes, turning once, until the tortillas are crisp and golden and the filling has melted. (If your pan is not big enough, you may have to do this one at a time.) Keep warm while you cook the remaining fold-overs. Place each fold-over on a warmed plate and serve with lots of green salad.

STU-SUPP-KIN

30 Bacon-Wrapped Pesto Chicken

Serves 4

4 skinless chicken breasts

3 tablespoons red or green pesto

125 g (4 oz) ball mozzarella, sliced

2 tomatoes, sliced

50 g (2 oz) young spinach leaves, washed

8 pancetta slices or rindless streaky bacon rashers

new potatoes and green vegetables, or tagliatelle and tomato-based sauce, to serve

- Slice the chicken breasts almost in half horizontally, then open up and spread the pesto all over both cut sides. Layer the mozzarella, tomatoes and spinach over the bottom half of each chicken breast, then fold over the top to cover the filling. Wrap each stuffed chicken breast in 2 slices of pancetta or bacon and arrange in an ovenproof dish.

- Cook in a preheated oven, 200°C (400°F), Gas Mark 6, for 20–25 minutes until cooked through and golden. Pierce the chicken with a skewer or sharp knife, to check that the juices run clear, then serve with new potatoes and green vegetables or tagliatelle with a tomato sauce.

10 Crispy Bacon and Pesto Pasta Salad

Heat 4 tablespoons olive oil in a frying pan and cook 8 chopped streaky bacon rashers or pancetta slices over a medium-high heat for 5–6 minutes until crisp and golden. Drain on kitchen paper. Meanwhile, cook 400 g (13 oz) quick-cook pasta in a pan of lightly salted boiling water for 3–5 minutes or according to the packet instructions until just tender. Drain and cool under running cold water. Mix 3 tablespoons red or green pesto with 3 tablespoons mayonnaise or crème fraîche and 1 tablespoon lemon juice. Mix the creamy pesto sauce into the pasta with 12 halved cherry tomatoes, then divide between 4 dishes and serve scattered with the bacon.

20 Wholewheat Pesto Spaghetti with Bacon

Cook 400 g (13 oz) wholewheat spaghetti in a pan of lightly salted boiling water for 10–12 minutes or according to the packet instructions until just tender. Meanwhile, heat 4 tablespoons olive oil in a large frying pan and cook 8 chopped streaky bacon rashers or pancetta slices over a medium-high heat for 4–5 minutes until lightly golden. Add 2 tablespoons pine nuts and 2 chopped garlic cloves to the pan and cook gently for a further 2 minutes, stirring frequently, until lightly golden. Stir 200 g (7 oz) finely chopped washed spinach leaves into the pan with 1 tablespoon lemon juice and stir frequently for 2–3 minutes until the spinach has wilted. Add 1 small bunch of roughly chopped basil leaves and remove from the heat. Drain the pasta, reserving 2 tablespoons of the cooking liquid, and return the pasta and reserved liquid to the pan. Scrape the chunky spinach-and-bacon pesto into the spaghetti with 2 tablespoons finely grated hard Italian cheese and toss quickly to combine. Heap into warmed bowls and serve immediately with extra grated cheese.

Grilled Gammon with Apple and Brie

Serves 4

1 tablespoon olive or vegetable oil

4 thick trimmed gammon steaks, about 175 g (6 oz) each

2 tablespoons apple sauce, plus extra to serve (optional)

125 g (4 oz) Brie, sliced

1 teaspoon dried thyme

green salad, to serve (optional)

- Rub the oil over the gammon steaks and arrange on the rack of a foil-lined grill tray. Cook under a grill preheated to a medium-hot setting for 4–5 minutes on each side until cooked through.

- Spread the apple sauce thinly over the grilled gammon and top with the sliced Brie and dried thyme. Return to the grill for a further 2–3 minutes until the cheese has melted and is golden.

- Serve with extra apple sauce and a green salad, if desired.

Apple, Brie and Ham Melts

Cut 1 ciabatta-style loaf in half and split each half across the middle to create 4 portions. Spread the cut side of each piece with 1 tablespoon apple sauce, then layer 50 g (2 oz) wafer-thin ham on top of each one. Divide 150 g (5 oz) sliced Brie between the ciabatta portions, then arrange on the rack of a foil-lined grill tray and cook under a grill preheated to a medium setting for 3–4 minutes until the cheese has melted. Serve with plenty of green salad.

Apple and Brie-Stuffed Pork

Cut a deep slash along the sides of 4 thick, boneless pork steaks to create a pocket in each one. Stuff each pocket with 1 teaspoon apple sauce and a thick slice of Brie, then sprinkle over 1 teaspoon dried thyme and wrap 2 slices of air-dried ham around each steak, covering the opening. Heat 2 tablespoons olive or vegetable oil in a frying pan and cook the pork chops over a medium-high heat for about 2 minutes on each side until the ham is golden. Transfer the pork chops to an ovenproof dish and pour over 125 ml (4 fl oz) dry cider or dry white wine. Place in a preheated oven, 180°C (350°F), Gas Mark 4, for 15–18 minutes until the pork is cooked through, but still juicy. Remove from the oven and serve with cooked broccoli or green beans and roast potatoes, if desired.

20 Poor Man's Pesto with Penne

Serves 4

50 g (2 oz) pumpkin seeds or
 walnuts
400 g (13 oz) wholewheat penne
70 g (3 oz) bag of rocket
1 small garlic clove, crushed
50 g (2 oz) Grana Padano cheese,
 freshly grated
75 ml (3 fl oz) olive or vegetable oil
salt and pepper

- Toast the pumpkin seeds or walnuts in a frying pan over a low heat for 3–4 minutes, shaking frequently. Tip the seeds or nuts onto a plate and set aside.

- Cook the penne in a pan of lightly salted boiling water for 11 minutes until tender, then drain.

- Meanwhile, finely chop the cooled seeds or nuts in a food processor with the rocket, garlic and cheese. Add the oil, pouring it in a steady stream, until thick and almost smooth (or make the pesto using a pestle and mortar or chop the ingredients by hand as finely as possible, then stir in the oil). Scrape into a bowl, season to taste and stir into the drained pasta to serve.

10 Poor Man's Pesto Pasta Salad

Cook 400 g (13 oz) quick-cook penne in a pan of boiling water for 4–5 minutes or according to the packet instructions until tender. Cool under running cold water, then drain. Meanwhile, make up the Poor Man's Pesto as above (or, alternatively, use 4 tablespoons shop-bought green pesto). Scrape into the pasta with 2 tablespoons lemon juice or balsamic vinegar, 200 g (7 oz) halved cherry tomatoes and a generous pinch of black pepper. Stir well to coat and serve with 100 g (3½ oz) crumbled feta, if desired.

30 Poor Man's Pesto Pasta Bake

Cook 300 g (10 oz) wholewheat penne in a pan of salted boiling water for 11 minutes or according to the packet instructions until tender. Drain. Meanwhile, make up the pesto as above. Stir in 250 g (8 oz) mascarpone or cream cheese and 3 diced tomatoes. Stir the sauce into the drained pasta and tip into a buttered ovenproof dish. Scatter over 3 tablespoons grated Grana Padano cheese, then cook in a preheated oven, 200°C (400°F), Gas Mark 6, for 15 minutes until bubbling and golden. Serve with green salad.

Smoked Bacon and Chicken Parcels

Serves 4

4 small chicken breasts

125 g (4 oz) smoked cheese or
mozzarella, sliced

1 small bunch of basil (optional)

8 smoked streaky bacon rashers

2 tablespoons olive or
vegetable oil

350 g (11½ oz) fresh tomato
and mascarpone pasta sauce
(or similar)

tagliatelle or selection of
vegetables, to serve

- Slice the chicken breasts almost in half horizontally, then stuff each pocket with the sliced cheese and 2–3 basil leaves, if using. Wrap the bacon around the chicken breasts to seal in the stuffing.

- Heat the oil in a frying pan and cook the chicken over a medium heat for 5–6 minutes on each side or until the bacon is golden and the chicken is thoroughly cooked. Pierce the chicken with a skewer or sharp knife, to check that the juices run clear, then remove from the pan and set aside to rest for 2–3 minutes.

- Meanwhile, gently warm the fresh sauce in the same pan, scraping any bits from the bottom of the pan. Serve the chicken parcels with cooked tagliatelle or vegetables and the warmed sauce.

Chicken, Ham and Cheese Parcels

Lay out 4 soft tortilla wraps and arrange 2 slices of wafer-thin cooked chicken breast and 50 g (2 oz) each of wafer-thin smoked ham, smoked cheese or mozzarella and drained and sliced roasted peppers in the centre of each tortilla. Top each with 2–3 basil leaves (optional) and fold the curved edges of each tortilla into the centre 4 times to create a square parcel. Heat a frying pan and toast the parcels, 2 at a time, for 1–2 minutes on each side. Serve hot with green salad.

Smoked Ham, Chicken and Cheese Puff Parcels

Roll a 500 g (1 lb) block of puff pastry into a large square measuring about 40 cm (16 inches). Cut into 4 individual squares and spread 2 teaspoons green or red pesto over each square. Arrange 2 slices of wafer-thin cooked chicken breast and 50 g (2 oz) each of smoked ham and smoked cheese or mozzarella in the centre of each square, then top with a small handful of rocket leaves. Now bring the corners of 1 square into the centre to envelope the filling and create a parcel. Twist the corners together to seal. Repeat with the remaining squares and arrange the parcels on a baking sheet. Brush with a little beaten egg and bake in a preheated oven, 200°C (400°F), Gas Mark 6, for 15–20 minutes until puffed up and golden. Serve on a bed of salad.

STU-SUPP-VYY

30 Classic Cheese Fondue

Serves 4

1 garlic clove, peeled and halved

200 ml (7 fl oz) dry white wine

2 teaspoons vinegar or lemon juice

1½ tablespoons cornflour

4 tablespoons kirsch, brandy, vodka or dry white wine

750 g (1½ lb) mixture of grated cheese (such as Emmental, Gruyère and mature Cheddar cheese)

selection of dippers, such as cubes of crusty bread, raw vegetables (carrot and celery sticks, broccoli and cauliflower florets, halved mushrooms, cherry tomatoes), cooked sausages, pickled onions, cornichons and new potatoes, to serve

- Rub the cut side of the garlic all over the inside of a saucepan, then discard. Pour in the wine and vinegar or lemon juice and bring to the boil. Meanwhile, stir the cornflour into the kirsch, brandy, vodka or wine until smooth.

- Reduce the heat slightly so that the wine is simmering gently, then pour the kirsch into the wine in a slow, steady drizzle, stirring constantly for 1–2 minutes until thickened slightly.

- Now stir in the cheese, a handful at a time, stirring constantly and waiting until the cheese has melted before adding more. Once all of the cheese has been combined and the fondue is smooth and thick, scrape into a warmed fondue dish and place on a lit fondue base following manufacturer's instructions. (Alternatively, transfer the saucepan directly to the table, placing it on a heatproof mat or board. You may need to reheat the pan gently from time to time as the fondue cools and thickens.)

- Serve the fondue with a selection of dippers.

 Quick Cheat's Fondue

Warm 700 g (1 lb 7 oz) chilled cheese pasta sauce in a large pan and stir in 200 g (7 oz) grated Cheddar cheese until melted. Scrape into a warmed fondue pot and serve with a selection of dippers, as above.

 Creamy Blue Cheese Fondue

Rub a pan with garlic, as above. Pour 250 ml (8 fl oz) dry white wine or cider into the pan and bring to the boil. Stir 1 tablespoon cornflour into 2 tablespoons wine or cider, then pour into the simmering pan in a slow, steady drizzle, stirring constantly until thickened. Add 500 g (1 lb) roughly diced creamy blue cheese (such as Saint Agur, Cambozola or dolcelatte) with 100 ml (3½ fl oz) double cream and stir frequently over a low heat until melted. Serve with a selection of dippers, as above.

10 Flaked Mackerel Salad with Lemon Dressing

Serves 4

2 tablespoons olive oil

300 g (10 oz) cooked new
potatoes, roughly sliced

2 x 125 g (4 oz) cans mackerel in
oil or brine, drained and flaked

150 g (5 oz) rocket salad or 4 little
gem lettuces, cut into wedges,
to serve

For the dressing

4 tablespoons lemon juice

2 tablespoons horseradish sauce
(optional)

150 ml (¼ pint) soured cream
or crème fraîche

salt and pepper

- Heat the oil in a large frying pan and fry the potatoes for 7–8 minutes, turning occasionally, until crisp and golden.

- Meanwhile, combine the dressing ingredients and season to taste.

- Divide the salad between 4 plates and flake over the mackerel in large chunks. Scatter over the golden potatoes and drizzle with the creamy lemon dressing to serve.

---

20 Lemony Mackerel Spaghetti

Cook 400 g (13 oz) spaghetti
in a pan of lightly salted water
for 11 minutes until tender.
Meanwhile, heat 4 tablespoons
olive oil in a small pan and add
2 chopped garlic cloves and
4 finely sliced spring onions.
Cook for 2–3 minutes over a low
heat. Stir in 250 g (8 oz) flaked
boneless and skinless smoked
mackerel fillets, 3 tablespoons
lemon juice and black pepper.
Take off the heat. Drain the
pasta, return to the pan and add
the lemony mackerel. Toss to
coat, then serve immediately.

30 Lemony Spinach and Mackerel Bake

Drain and thickly slice 2 x 400 g
(13 oz) cans new potatoes and
tip into a large pan with 250 g
(8 oz) flaked boneless and
skinless smoked mackerel,
3 finely sliced spring onions
(optional), 300 ml (½ pint)
soured cream, the grated rind
and juice of 1 lemon and 150 g
(5 oz) defrosted leaf spinach.
Mix gently and heat over a low
heat for 3–4 minutes, then tip
into an ovenproof dish and
scatter over 125 g (4 oz) grated
Cheddar cheese (or similar).
Bake in a preheated oven,

200°C (400°F), Gas Mark 6, for
20–22 minutes until golden and
bubbling. Serve with a rocket
and leaf salad.

 # Turkey Tikka Skewers

Serves 4

3 tablespoons tikka masala
  curry paste
2 tablespoons natural yogurt
500 g (1 lb) diced turkey breast
1 large onion, cut into bite-sized
  pieces
1 large green pepper, cut into
  bite-sized pieces

To serve

cooked basmati or long-grain rice
mango chutney (optional)

- In a bowl, mix the curry paste with the yogurt, then add the diced turkey. Mix well to coat, then thread onto 4–8 metal or soaked wooden skewers with the chunks of onion and pepper. Arrange on the rack of a foil-lined grill tray.

- Cook under a grill that has been preheated to a medium setting for 12–15 minutes, turning occasionally, until thoroughly cooked and lightly charred.

- Serve hot with cooked rice and mango chutney, if desired.

---

10 Tandoori Turkey Steaks with Rice

Sprinkle 3 tablespoons tandoori spice blend or tandoori curry powder over 8 quick-cook turkey breast steaks. Heat 2 tablespoons vegetable oil in a large non-stick frying pan and cook the turkey steaks for 2–3 minutes on each side or until cooked through. Meanwhile, heat 500 g (1 lb) cooked basmati or long-grain rice according to the packet instructions or in a frying pan with 1 tablespoon oil, stir-frying for 4–5 minutes until hot. (If you are cooking the rice when making this recipe, you'll need 300 g/10 oz uncooked rice.) Spoon the hot rice onto warmed plates and serve with the tandoori turkey steaks and mango chutney, if desired.

---

30 Turkey Tikka Masala

Heat 2 tablespoons vegetable oil in a large saucepan and cook 1 large roughly chopped onion and 1 diced green or red pepper for 7–8 minutes until softened. Stir 4 tablespoons tikka masala curry paste into the pan followed by 400 g (13 oz) diced turkey breast. Stir to combine and seal the turkey, then add a 400 g (13 oz) can chopped tomatoes and 300 ml (½ pint) water. Bring to the boil, then reduce the heat and simmer gently, uncovered, for 12–15 minutes until the turkey is thoroughly cooked and the sauce has thickened. Stir 125 g (4 oz) full-fat natural yogurt into the curry before serving with plenty of cooked basmati or long-grain rice.

3⬤ Margherita Tart

Serves 4

375 g (12 oz) sheet of pre-rolled
  puff pastry
3 tablespoons green or red pesto
300 g (10 oz) cherry tomatoes,
  halved (or regular tomatoes,
  sliced)
125 g (4 oz) mozzarella cheese,
  torn or sliced
12 pitted green or black olives
  in brine, rinsed and drained
  (optional)
1 teaspoon dried oregano
  (optional)
2 teaspoons olive oil
rocket salad, to serve (optional)

- Unroll the sheet of pastry on a lined or lightly greased baking sheet and lightly score a 1.5 cm (¾ inch) border around the edge.

- Spread the pesto evenly over the base, working within the border. Arrange the cherry tomatoes and mozzarella over the pesto, then scatter over the olives and oregano, if using.

- Drizzle with the oil and bake in a preheated oven, 190°C (375°F), Gas Mark 5, for 20–25 minutes until the pastry is crisp and golden. Cut into squares and serve with a rocket salad, if desired.

1⬤ **Margherita Salad**
Divide 150 g (5 oz) rocket leaves and 300 g (10 oz) halved cherry tomatoes or sliced tomatoes between 4 large plates. Scatter over 250 g (8 oz) torn mozzarella and 12 pitted olives (optional), then top with ½ very thinly sliced red onion. Make a dressing by placing 2 teaspoons of red or green pesto in a small bowl or jar and adding 1½ tablespoons balsamic vinegar and 3 tablespoons olive oil. Mix well to combine, then drizzle over the salads to serve.

2⬤ **Margherita Pizza**
Spread 4 mini pizza bases or 2 large pizza bases with 6 tablespoons pizza topping sauce, leaving a 1 cm (½ inch) border. Scatter over 250 g (8 oz) sliced mozzarella and 125 g (4 oz) halved cherry tomatoes. Top with 12 pitted olives and ½ teaspoon dried oregano, if desired, then drizzle over 2 teaspoons olive oil and bake in a preheated oven, 200°C (400°F), Gas Mark 6, for 12–15 minutes until crisp and golden. Serve with green salad, if desired.

20 Barbecue Pork Steaks with Corn and Rice

Serves 4

2 spring onions, thinly sliced,
  plus extra to garnish (optional)
4 tablespoons sticky barbecue
  marinade
4 trimmed pork steaks, about
  125 g (4 oz) each
300 g (10 oz) long-grain rice
8 frozen mini corn on the cob

- Mix the spring onion with the barbecue marinade, then rub the mixture over the pork steaks. Arrange in a shallow ovenproof dish and marinate in the refrigerator for 10 minutes.

- Cook under a grill preheated to a medium-hot setting for 6–8 minutes, turning and basting occasionally, or until cooked through but still juicy.

- Meanwhile, cook the rice in a pan of lightly salted boiling water for about 15 minutes or according to the packet instructions until tender. Drain well.

- Cook the frozen mini corn on the cobs in a separate pan of boiling water for 6–7 minutes or according to the packet instructions until just tender. Drain well.

- Spoon the rice into 4 warmed dishes, then top with the pork and any barbecue juices and serve with the corn, garnished with extra spring onions, if desired.

10 Chinese-Style Barbecue Pork Pot

Noodles Heat 2 tablespoons vegetable oil in a frying pan and stir-fry 400 g (13 oz) stir-fry pork strips for 3–4 minutes until cooked through. Add 150 g (5 oz) shredded mangetout and stir-fry for 1 minute, then stir in 400 g (13 oz) cooked egg noodles. Stir occasionally for 2–3 minutes until hot, then pour a 195 g (7 oz) jar of hoi sin sauce into the pan. Once hot, heap into bowls and serve.

30 Sticky Barbecue Pork with Wedges

In a bowl, mix 4 tablespoons tomato ketchup with 2 crushed garlic cloves, 2 tablespoons honey, 2 tablespoons dark soft brown sugar, 2 teaspoons Worcestershire sauce, 1 tablespoon red wine vinegar, 1 tablespoon dark soy sauce and 1 tablespoon vegetable oil. (Alternatively, use 6 tablespoons sticky barbecue marinade.) Rub the marinade all over 4 lean pork steaks, about 150 g (5 oz)

each, and marinate in the refrigerator for 10 minutes. Heat 1 tablespoon vegetable oil in a large non-stick frying pan and cook the steaks gently for 12–15 minutes, turning and basting frequently, until cooked through and sticky. Meanwhile, cook 500 g (1 lb) frozen potato wedges according to the packet instructions until golden. Serve the sticky pork with the potato wedges and cooked corn on the cob, if desired.

 # Creamy Curried Prawns

Serves 4

50 g (2 oz) butter
1 small onion, thinly sliced
2.5 cm (1 inch) piece of fresh
 root ginger, peeled and finely
 chopped (optional)
3 tablespoons mild curry paste
 (such as korma paste)
400 ml (14 fl oz) coconut milk
300 g (10 oz) raw or cooked
 peeled prawns
small bunch of coriander, roughly
 chopped
cooked long-grain or basmati
 rice, to serve

- Melt the butter in a large frying pan and cook the onion and ginger, if using, for 7–8 minutes over a gentle heat so as not burn the butter, stirring occasionally, until the onion is soft.

- Stir in the curry paste and cook, stirring, for a further 1–2 minutes to cook the spices. Stir in the coconut milk and bring to the boil. Reduce the heat, cover and simmer gently for 7–8 minutes.

- If using raw prawns, stir them into the pan for the final 2–3 minutes of cooking – they should be cooked through and pink. Alternatively, stir through cooked prawns for the final minute until hot. Remove from the heat and scatter over the chopped coriander, then serve immediately, spooned over cooked rice.

 Coronation Prawn Wraps

Mix 2 tablespoons natural yogurt with 2 tablespoons mayonnaise, 1 teaspoon mild curry powder, 1 tablespoon smooth mango chutney and 1 teaspoon lemon juice. Season with salt and pepper, then stir in 300 g/10 oz cooked peeled prawns (or 300 g /10 oz sliced cooked chicken). Stir well, then spoon onto 4 large or 8 small soft tortilla wraps and scatter over a small bunch of chopped coriander (optional). Add shredded Iceberg lettuce and 4–5 cucumber slices cucumber (optional), then wrap tightly and halve to serve.

 Aromatic Prawn Pilau

Heat 2 tablespoons vegetable oil in a large frying pan and cook 1 finely chopped onion, 1 tablespoon peeled and chopped fresh root ginger and 2 chopped garlic cloves over a medium heat for 7–8 minutes until softened. Stir in 2 tablespoons mild curry paste for 1 minute, then stir 300 g (10 oz) long-grain rice into the pan. Pour in 700 ml (1¼ pint) hot chicken or vegetable stock and bring to the boil, then reduce the heat, cover and simmer gently for about 15 minutes until the rice is tender and the liquid has been

absorbed. Fluff up the rice with a fork, fold through 300 g (10 oz) cooked peeled prawns, then cover and set aside for 2–3 minutes until the prawns are hot. Serve scattered with chopped coriander, if desired.

30 One-Pan Sausage Roast

Serves 4

8 Cumberland sausages

1 onion, cut into wedges

400 g (13 oz) small new potatoes, halved, or new potatoes, cut into wedges

2 large carrots, washed and cut into chunks

2 rosemary sprigs or 1 teaspoon dried rosemary

3 tablespoons olive or vegetable oil

salt and pepper

Yorkshire puddings and gravy, to serve (optional)

- Place the sausages in a large roasting pan and add the remaining ingredients. Mix well to coat everything in the oil and seasoning and spread out in the pan in a single layer.

- Roast in a preheated oven, 200°C (400°F), Gas Mark 6, for 20–25 minutes, turning occasionally, until the sausages are cooked and golden and the vegetables are tender.

- Serve hot with golden Yorkshire puddings and a jug of hot gravy, if desired.

 1 One-Pan Sausage Omelette

Heat 2 tablespoons olive or vegetable oil in a frying pan and add 2 x 300 g (10 oz) cans new potatoes, drained and sliced, 3 sliced spring onions and 225 g (7½ oz) cooked smoked sausage, sliced. Toss over a medium-high heat for 2 minutes until hot. Meanwhile, beat 6 eggs in a bowl with a pinch each of salt and pepper, then pour into the pan. Stir to combine, then cook gently for 4–5 minutes until almost set. Scatter over 125 g (4 oz) grated Cheddar cheese and slide the pan under a hot grill, keeping the handle away from the heat. Grill for 2 minutes until golden and bubbling. Serve with green salad.

 2 One-Pan Sausage Casserole

Heat 2 tablespoons olive or vegetable oil in a large saucepan and cook 1 halved and thinly sliced onion and 1 trimmed and finely sliced celery stick over a medium heat for 6–7 minutes to soften. Add 2 chopped garlic cloves and 2 teaspoons ground cumin (optional) and cook for a further 1–2 minutes until the garlic is just softened. Stir a 400 g (13 oz) can chopped tomatoes into the pan with a 400 g (13 oz) can drained and rinsed chickpeas or haricot beans, then bring to the boil and simmer for about 8 minutes, adding 150 g (5 oz) washed spinach for the final minute.

Stir in 200 g (7 oz) cooked bite-sized snack or cocktail sausages and stir for a further minute until hot. Spoon into 4 deep bowls and serve with crusty bread and chopped parsley, if desired.

30 Creamy Mushroom and Chive Risotto

Serves 4

50 g (2 oz) butter
1 onion, finely chopped
2 garlic cloves, finely chopped
300 g (10 oz) mushrooms, preferably brown-cap, chopped
350 g (11½ oz) risotto rice
125 ml (4 fl oz) dry white wine (optional)
1.2 litres (2 pints) hot chicken or vegetable stock (add an extra 125 ml/4 fl oz if not using wine)
3 tablespoons crème fraîche
2 tablespoons chopped chives
salt and pepper
grated hard Italian cheese, to serve (optional)

- Melt the butter in a pan and cook the onion and garlic over a medium heat for 4–5 minutes. Add the mushrooms and cook for 2–3 minutes, stirring occasionally. Add the risotto rice and stir for 1 minute. Pour in the white wine, if using, and simmer rapidly for about 1 minute until the wine is absorbed.

- Add a small ladleful of hot stock. Stir constantly and keep the mixture at a gentle simmer. When the liquid has been absorbed, repeat the process. Continue for about 17 minutes until all the stock has been absorbed and the rice is tender and creamy, but with texture.

- Stir the crème fraîche and chives into the risotto, season generously, remove from the heat, cover and set aside for 2 minutes. Serve sprinkled with grated hard Italian cheese.

---

1 Grilled Mushrooms with Polenta and Chives

Arrange 8–12 large flat field mushrooms, trimmed, in a shallow ovenproof dish and place a slice of garlic butter, about 15 g (½ oz), on the cut side of each one. Cook under a grill preheated to a medium setting for about 5–6 minutes until softened. Meanwhile, bring 750 ml (1¼ pints) hot chicken or vegetable stock to the boil in a large pan. Pour 200 g (7 oz) quick-cook polenta into the pan in a slow steady stream, stirring constantly with a wooden spoon or whisk, until thickened. Reduce the heat and simmer gently for 2 minutes. Stir in 50 g (2 oz) garlic butter and 3 tablespoons finely chopped chives. Spoon into 4 warmed dishes, then top with the mushrooms and their juices and serve immediately with grated hard Italian cheese, if desired.

2 Creamy Mushroom and Chive Linguine

Cook 400 g (13 oz) linguine in lightly salted boiling water for 11 minutes until tender. Meanwhile, heat 25 g (1 oz) butter with 1 tablespoon oil in a frying pan and cook 1 chopped onion for 7–8 minutes. Add 300 g (10 oz) chopped field mushrooms with 2 chopped garlic cloves and cook for 3–4 minutes, stirring occasionally. Pour 300 ml (½ pint) single cream into the pan with 3 tablespoons chopped chives. Season with salt and pepper. Boil, stir in 1 tablespoon lemon juice, then toss through the drained linguine to serve.

20 Breaded Fish with Mushy Peas

Serves 4

500 g (1 lb) oven chips
2–3 tablespoons plain flour
1 large egg, beaten
6 tablespoons dried breadcrumbs
4 boneless, skinless white fish
  fillets, about 125 g (4 oz) each
4 tablespoons vegetable oil
250 g (8 oz) frozen peas
1 tablespoon lemon juice
2 tablespoons crème fraîche
  (optional)
salt and pepper
tartare sauce, to serve (optional)

- Arrange the chips on a baking sheet and cook in a preheated oven, 220°C (425°F), Gas Mark 7, for 15–18 minutes or according to the packet instructions until golden. Meanwhile, place the flour, egg and breadcrumbs in 3 separate shallow dishes. Season the flour. Dust each fish fillet in flour, then dip into the beaten egg, turning to coat. Now turn in the breadcrumbs to coat.

- Heat the oil in a frying pan and shallow-fry the fish over a medium heat for 3–4 minutes on each side until the coating is golden and crunchy and the fish is cooked through.

- Meanwhile, cook the peas in a pan of boiling water for 3–5 minutes until tender. Take off the heat, drain and mash with the lemon juice, crème fraîche, if using, salt and pepper (or tip the peas, lemon juice and crème fraîche into a food processor and pulse until mushy). Serve the crispy breaded fish with the golden oven chips, mushy peas, lemon wedges and tartare sauce, if desired.

 Grilled Fish Fingers with Peas

Cook 8–12 fish fingers under a grill preheated to a medium-hot setting for about 8 minutes, turning occasionally. Meanwhile, boil 400 g (13 oz) frozen peas for 3–5 minutes. Drain and return to the pan. Add 50 g (2 oz) butter, salt and pepper and 1 tablespoon mint sauce or 1 teaspoon finely chopped mint and stir. Serve topped with the grilled fish fingers with tartare sauce or ketchup and buttered brown bread.

 Herby Crust Fish with Mash

In a bowl, combine 75 g (3 oz) fresh breadcrumbs with 1 teaspoon finely grated lemon rind (optional), 2 tablespoons finely chopped parsley, 1 tablespoon finely chopped chives and a pinch each of salt and pepper. Rub a little oil over the fish fillets and press them into the breadcrumb mixture to coat lightly. Arrange in an ovenproof dish or baking sheet and top with the remaining breadcrumb mixture. Place in a preheated oven, 200°C (400°F), Gas Mark 6, for 15–20 minutes or until the crust is golden and the fish is flaky. Meanwhile, cook 750 g (1½ lb) peeled and diced potatoes in a pan of boiling water for 12–15 minutes until tender. Drain and mash with 50 g (2 oz) butter and a splash of milk. Season to taste, spoon onto 4 warmed plates and serve with the golden fish and some cooked peas, if desired.

1 Green Curry Noodle Soup

Serves 4

200 ml (7 fl oz) coconut milk

1–2 tablespoons Thai green
curry paste

900 ml (1½ pints) hot chicken
or vegetable stock

2 tablespoons fish sauce or
lime juice

175 g (6 oz) mangetout or fine
green beans, sliced

300 g (10 oz) cooked medium
noodles

- Pour the coconut milk into a large saucepan and bring to the boil. Stir in the curry paste and simmer for 1–2 minutes before adding the hot chicken or vegetable stock and fish sauce or lime juice.

- Simmer gently for 5 minutes, then stir in the mangetout or green beans and noodles. Cook for 3–4 minutes until just tender, then ladle into bowls and serve immediately.

2 Green Vegetable Curry

Heat 3 tablespoons vegetable oil in a frying pan and add 1 diced aubergine and 1 sliced onion. Cook over a medium-high heat for 5 minutes, stirring frequently, until lightly coloured and beginning to soften. Reduce the heat and stir in 2 tablespoons Thai green curry paste, 400 ml (14 fl oz) coconut milk and 300 ml (½ pint) hot chicken or vegetable stock. Bring to the boil, simmer gently for 5 minutes, then add 150 g (5 oz) green beans and 200 g (7 oz) broccoli florets and cook for a further 6–7 minutes until tender. Stir in 1 tablespoon fish sauce or lime juice and serve over bowls of cooked rice, garnished with coriander leaves, if desired.

3 Sweet Potato and Green Bean Curry

Heat 2 tablespoons vegetable oil in a large frying pan or saucepan and add 1 roughly chopped onion, 300 g (10 oz) peeled and diced sweet potato and 1 diced aubergine. Cook over a medium heat for 7–8 minutes, stirring frequently, until the onion is softened. Add a 2.5 cm (1 inch) piece of fresh root ginger, peeled and chopped, and 2 chopped garlic cloves and cook for a further 2–3 minutes until softened. Stir in 2 tablespoons Thai red curry paste, 400 ml (14 fl oz) coconut milk and 400 ml (14 fl oz) hot vegetable stock and bring to the boil. Reduce the heat and simmer gently for 7–8 minutes to allow the flavours to develop. Add 150 g (5 oz) green beans and 1 thinly sliced red pepper, then simmer for a further 7–8 minutes until all the vegetables are tender. Stir in 1 tablespoon fish sauce or lime juice, then spoon over bowls of cooked rice and garnish with coriander leaves, if desired, to serve.

STU-SUPP-POP

30 Roasted Peppers with Mozzarella and Couscous

Serves 4

4 large red peppers, tops
  removed, cored (but left whole)

2 garlic cloves, sliced

2 x 125 g (4 oz) balls mozzarella,
  halved

1 teaspoon chilli flakes (optional)

12 cherry tomatoes

2 tablespoons olive or
  vegetable oil

250 g (8 oz) flavoured couscous

25 g (1 oz) butter

300 ml (½ pint) boiling vegetable
  or chicken stock

rocket leaves, to serve (optional)

- Arrange the cored red peppers in a shallow ovenproof dish and stuff each one with a few slices of garlic, ½ a ball of mozzarella, a pinch of chilli flakes, if using, and 3 cherry tomatoes. Drizzle with the oil and roast in a preheated oven, 200°C (400°F), Gas Mark 6, for 20–25 minutes until softened.

- Meanwhile, place the couscous in a bowl with the butter and pour over the boiling stock. Cover and set aside for 6–8 minutes until the liquid has been absorbed and the grains are tender. Fluff with a fork and spoon onto serving plates. Top with a roasted pepper and serve with the rocket, if using.

 Quick Pepper and Mozzarella Salad

Arrange 4 quartered peppers on the rack of a foil-lined grill tray, skin side up, and drizzle over 2 tablespoons olive or vegetable oil. Cook under a grill preheated to hot for 6–7 minutes until softened and lightly charred. Cool slightly, then slice thickly. Meanwhile, spoon 500 g (1 lb) prepared couscous salad into 4 dishes and top each one with a small handful of rocket leaves. Tear 2 x 125 g (4 oz) balls of mozzarella and scatter over the rocket leaves. Top with the sliced peppers and serve immediately with a drizzle each of olive oil and balsamic vinegar.

 Grilled Pepper and Cheese Couscous

Arrange 4 halved and cored red or yellow peppers, cut side up, on the rack of a foil-lined grill tray and divide 250 g (8 oz) drained mini mozzarella balls or diced mozzarella between them. Top each half with a pinch each of chilli flakes and chopped garlic. Drizzle 2 tablespoons olive or vegetable oil over the peppers and cook under a grill preheated to a medium-low setting for 8–10 minutes or until the cheese is melting and lightly charred. Meanwhile, cook the couscous as above. Spoon onto serving plates and serve topped with the peppers.

Gingery Grilled Tofu with Noodles

Serves 4

2 tablespoons vegetable oil

about 500 g (1 lb) prepared stir-fry vegetables

410 g (13⅓ oz) chilled fresh noodles

400 g (13 oz) firm tofu, thickly sliced

For the marinade

2.5 cm (1 inch) piece of fresh root ginger, peeled and grated

2 large garlic cloves, crushed

3 tablespoons dark soy sauce

3 tablespoons clear honey

- Heat the oil in a wok and stir-fry the vegetables for 3–4 minutes. Add the noodles and toss for a further 3–4 minutes.

- Meanwhile, mix together the ginger, garlic, soy and honey. Add the sliced tofu and turn gently in the marinade to coat. Reserve the remaining marinade. Arrange the tofu on a foil-lined baking sheet and cook under a grill preheated to a medium setting for about 4 minutes, carefully turning once, until golden.

- Remove the noodles from the heat, drizzle over the remaining marinade and serve topped with the grilled tofu.

2 Gingery Tofu Stir-Fry

Heat 2 tablespoons oil in a wok and stir-fry 320 g (10¾ oz) marinated tofu pieces for 3–4 minutes. Remove and set aside. Add 500 g (1 lb) prepared stir-fry vegetables to the pan and stir-fry for 3–4 minutes until just tender. Add a 2.5 cm (1 inch) piece peeled and chopped fresh root ginger and 2 chopped garlic cloves and stir-fry for 1 minute. Meanwhile, mix 3 tablespoons light soy sauce with 2 tablespoons clear honey, then remove the pan from the heat, pour over the sauce and return the tofu to the pan. Toss to coat and serve with 500 g (1 lb) egg-fried rice.

3 Ginger Marinated Tofu and Vegetable Parcels

In a bowl, mix 4 tablespoons light soy sauce with 2 tablespoons sesame or vegetable oil, 2 tablespoons honey, 1 tablespoon peeled and grated fresh root ginger, 2 crushed garlic cloves and 3 finely sliced spring onions. Thickly slice 800 g (1 lb 10 oz) firm tofu and toss gently in the marinade to coat. Set aside for 10 minutes. Meanwhile, cut 4 large circles from baking paper and 4 large circles from kitchen foil. Lay each paper circle on top of a foil one. Divide about 500 g (1 lb) prepared stir-fry vegetables between the circles.

Top the vegetables with slices of marinated tofu, then drizzle over the remaining marinade. Bring up the sides of the foil-and-paper lining and scrunch the edges together to seal. Arrange on a large baking sheet and place in a preheated oven, 200°C (400°F), Gas Mark 6, for 12–15 minutes until the vegetables are just tender. Place the parcels directly onto 4 warmed plates to serve.

30 Vegetable Curry with Rice

Serves 4

2 tablespoons vegetable oil

1 onion, roughly chopped

600 g (1 lb 3½ oz) mixed chopped vegetables (such as carrots, leeks, swede, potato, cauliflower and broccoli)

2 garlic cloves, chopped

2.5 cm (1 inch) piece of fresh root ginger, peeled and chopped

4 tablespoons medium-hot curry paste (such as rogan josh or balti)

400 g (13 oz) can chopped tomatoes

400 ml (14 fl oz) hot vegetable stock

cooked rice, to serve

- Heat the oil in a large frying pan and cook the onion and mixed vegetables over a medium heat for about 10 minutes, stirring frequently, until lightly coloured and beginning to soften. Stir in the garlic and ginger for a further 2 minutes, then add the curry paste and stir over the heat for 1 minute to cook the spices.

- Pour in the chopped tomatoes and vegetable stock, then bring to the boil, reduce the heat and simmer gently for about 15 minutes until the curry has thickened slightly and the vegetables are tender. Serve spooned over cooked rice.

 Vegetable Rice with Curry Sauce

Heat 2 tablespoons oil in a pan and stir-fry 500 g (1 lb) cooked pilau rice for 3–4 minutes until piping hot. Stir in 2 x 300 g (10 oz) cans mixed vegetables, drained, or 400 g (13 oz) cooked and diced mixed vegetables, and stir into the rice for 2–3 minutes until hot. Meanwhile, heat a 500 g (1 lb) jar of curry sauce in a small pan, stirring occasionally, for 2–3 minutes until almost boiling. Remove from the heat. Spoon the vegetable rice into warmed bowls and serve with the hot curry sauce and warmed naan bread, if desired.

 Curried Vegetable and Rice Bowl

Heat 2 tablespoons oil in a large frying pan and cook 1 chopped onion and 1 chopped pepper over a medium-high heat for 3–4 minutes until lightly coloured and beginning to soften. Add 2 chopped garlic cloves and 1 tablespoon peeled and chopped fresh root ginger and cook for 1 minute, then add 3 tablespoons hot curry paste (such as Madras paste) and cook for 1 minute. Pour a 400 g (13 oz) can chopped tomatoes into the pan with 2 teaspoons wine vinegar and 250 ml (8 fl oz) hot vegetable stock or water.

Bring to the boil, then reduce the heat and simmer gently for 6–7 minutes. Stir in 400 g (13 oz) frozen mixed vegetables and simmer gently for a further 5–6 minutes until just tender. Spoon over bowls of hot pilau rice to serve.

Fisherman's Sardine and Potato Salad

Serves 4

3 tablespoons mayonnaise

2 tablespoons tartare sauce

2 teaspoons lemon juice

2 tablespoons chopped chives
or parsley (optional)

625 g (1¼ lb) cooked potatoes,
diced

2 x 120 g (3¾ oz) cans sardines,
drained and flaked

salt and pepper

• In a large bowl, mix the mayonnaise, tartare sauce, lemon juice and chopped herbs and season with a pinch each of salt and pepper.

• Fold through the potatoes and flaked sardines and divide between serving plates.

2 Fisherman's Sardine Linguine

Cook 400 g (13 oz) linguine or spaghetti in a pan of lightly salted boiling water for about 11 minutes or according to the packet instructions until tender. Meanwhile, heat 3 tablespoons olive oil in a frying pan and gently cook 2 chopped garlic cloves and 1 deseeded and finely chopped red chilli for 2–3 minutes. Take off the heat and stir in the grated rind and juice of 1 lemon, 1 small bunch of chopped parsley and 2 x 120 g (3¾ oz) cans sardines in tomato sauce (or use canned crab, tuna or salmon). Season to taste. Drain the pasta, return it to the pan and add the sardine mixture to the pasta. Toss briefly over a medium heat, then serve.

3 Fisherman's Pie with Sardines

Heat 700 g (1 lb 7 oz) fresh tomato-based pasta sauce (such as arrabbiata or Napoletana) in a large pan. Add 390 g (12½ oz) fish pie mix (or mixed chunks of salmon, haddock and smoked haddock) and simmer gently for 5–8 minutes until the fish is just cooked and flaky. Flake in a 120 g (3¾ oz) can sardines in tomato sauce and 200 g (7 oz) cooked peeled prawns, then tip into a shallow ovenproof dish. In a small bowl, mix 75 g (3 oz) coarse breadcrumbs with 2 tablespoons finely grated hard Italian cheese (optional), 2 tablespoons finely chopped parsley or chives (optional) and 1 tablespoon olive oil. Mix well to coat, then sprinkle over the fish and bake in a preheated oven, 190°C (375°F), Gas Mark 5, for about 15 minutes until golden and crispy. Serve immediately with your preferred vegetables, if desired.

QuickCook
Sweet Fix

Recipes listed by cooking time

30

Banoffee Chocolate
Muffins   232

Mixed Dried Fruit
Rock Cakes   234

Vanilla and Raspberry
Jam Sponge Cake   236

Coconut Rice Pudding
with Pineapple   238

Chocolate Orange
Cheesecake   240

White Chocolate and
Apricot Muffins   242

Berry Good Crumble   244

Chocolate Bar
Brownie Buns   246

Chewy Oat and
Raisin Bars   248

Roasted Rhubarb Crunch   250

Frozen Fruit Pudding   252

Saucy Chocolate Pudding   254

Storecupboard Apricot
and Almond Crumble   256

Rum and Raisin Crêpes
with Ice Cream   258

Warm Cranberry-
Poached Pears   260

Lemon Popping
Candy Cakes   262

Upside-Down
Mandarin Muffins   264

Vanilla and Banana Cakes   266

Fruit Salad
Frozen Yogurt   268

Cherry Jam Swiss Roll   270

Classic Ginger Biscuits
with Stewed Apple   272

Peachy Cinnamon
Cheesecake   274

Sweet and Sticky
Raisin Pudding   276

Easy Chocolate Cake   278

20

Boozy Banana
Chocolate Trifle   232

Mixed Dried Fruit
Scones   234

Vanilla and Raspberry
Fairy Cakes   236

Pineapple Baked
Rice Pudding   238

Chocolate Orange Pots   240

Poached Apricots   242

Very Berry Tarts   244

Milk Chocolate Chip
Cookies   246

Coconut and Raisin
Oat Cookies   248

Stewed Rhubarb
with Custard   250

Frozen Fruit Cakes   252

Chocolate Buttermilk
Pancakes   254

Apricot and Almond
Tartlets   256

Rum, Raisin and
Pear Trifle   258

Quick Pear and
Cranberry Crumble   260

10

Lemon Sorbet Cakes	262
White Chocolate Mandarin Nests	264
Baked Bananas with Vanilla Cream	266
Fruit Salad Tartlets	268
Swiss Roll Cherry Bites	270
Apple and Ginger Baked Meringues	272
Cinnamon Pain Perdu with Peaches	274
Sweet and Sticky Apple and Raisin Tart	276
Easy Chocolate Cupcakes	278

Banoffee Chocolate Sundaes	232
Mixed Dried Fruit Compote with Ice Cream	234
Vanilla and Raspberry Sponge Trifle	236
Golden Pineapple with Rice Pudding	238
Chocolate Orange Milkshake	240
White Chocolate and Apricot Waffles	242
Berry-Full Baskets	244
Chocolate Bar Fondue	246
Crunchy Strawberry, Oat and Raisin Fool	248
Rhubarb and Custard Sponge Tart	250
Frozen Fruit Sponge Slice	252
Hot Chocolate Custard Brownies	254
Apricot and Amaretti Crumbles	256
Ice Cream with Rum and Raisin Syrup	258
Crunchy Pear and Cranberry Pots	260

Lemon Cupcake Surprise	262
Mandarin Eton Mess	264
Vanilla and Banana Yogurt	266
Fresh Fruit Salad	268
Chocolate Cherry Swiss Roll Trifle	270
Apple and Ginger Crunch Cream	272
Peachy Cinnamon Smoothie	274
Sweet and Sticky Raisin Waffles	276
Easy Chocolate Sauce for Ice Cream	278

30 Banoffee Chocolate Muffins

Serves 6

225 g (7½ oz) self-raising flour, sifted

2 tablespoons cocoa powder, sifted

100 g (3½ oz) caster sugar

100 g (3½ oz) dark chocolate chips

2 eggs

2 small ripe bananas, mashed

50 ml (2 fl oz) vegetable oil

125 g (4 oz) natural yogurt

warmed toffee sauce, to serve

- In a bowl, mix together the flour, cocoa powder, caster sugar and 75 g (3 oz) of the chocolate chips.

- Combine the eggs, bananas, oil and yogurt in a jug or bowl, then pour the wet ingredients into the dry and mix to barely combine. Divide the mixture between the greased or paper case-lined cups of a 12-cup muffin tin and scatter over the remaining chocolate chips.

- Bake in the preheated oven, 180°C (350°F), Gas Mark 4, for 18–22 minutes until risen and firm to the touch. Cool slightly on wire racks and serve warm, drizzled with warm toffee sauce.

---

 1 Banoffee Chocolate Sundaes

Crumble 12 chocolate cream sandwich biscuits (such as Oreos) into the bottom of 6 sundae glasses and drizzle 1 tablespoon toffee or caramel sauce over each one. Slice 3 large ripe, but firm, bananas and scatter them over the toffee sauce. Top each sundae with 2 scoops of ice cream and finish with a squirt of whipped cream. Drizzle with a little extra sauce to serve, if desired.

 2 Boozy Banana Chocolate Trifle

Thickly slice 3 large shop-bought (or leftover homemade) chocolate muffins (slightly stale is fine) and arrange the slices across the base of a large glass bowl or trifle dish. Drizzle over 75 ml (3 fl oz) Irish cream liqueur (such as Baileys) and set aside to soak. Meanwhile, slice 3 large ripe, but firm, bananas and whip 200 ml (7 fl oz) double cream to soft peaks. Scatter the bananas over the muffins, drizzle with 4 tablespoons toffee sauce and top with the softly whipped cream. Scatter over a mixture of dried banana and chocolate chips, to decorate.

1 Mixed Dried Fruit Compote with Ice Cream

Serves 4–6

250 g (8 oz) mixed chunky
  dried fruit, such as apricots,
  prunes, dates etc.
350 ml (12 fl oz) orange juice
1 vanilla pod, split
8–12 scoops vanilla ice cream
ice cream wafers, to serve
  (optional)

- Place the dried fruits in a small pan with the orange juice and vanilla pod and simmer gently for 6–7 minutes, stirring frequently, until the fruits have swollen and softened.

- Scrape into a bowl and set aside to cool slightly. Meanwhile, arrange the ice cream between 4–6 bowls then spoon over the warm dried fruit compote with any juices. Serve with wafers, if desired.

2 Mixed Dried Fruit Scones

Place 300 g (10 oz) self-raising flour and 2 teaspoons baking powder in a bowl and rub in 75 g (3 oz) softened butter until the mixture resembles breadcrumbs. Stir in 50 g (2 oz) mixed dried fruit and 2 tablespoons caster sugar. Combine 125 ml (4 fl oz) milk with 1 large lightly beaten egg, then pour into the bowl and mix to a soft dough. Tip onto a lightly floured surface and gently flatten the dough to a thickness of about 1.5 cm (¾ inch). Stamp out about 12 scones using a 5 cm (2 inch) cutter, then arrange on a lightly greased baking tray and brush lightly with a little milk. Bake in a preheated oven, 200°C, (400°F), Gas Mark 6, for about 12 minutes until risen and golden. Transfer to wire racks to cool slightly. Makes about 12 scones.

3 Mixed Dried Fruit Rock Cakes

Sift 250 g (8 oz) self-raising flour into a large bowl with 2 teaspoons baking powder and 1 teaspoon ground cinnamon (optional). Rub 125 g (4 oz) softened butter into the flour until the mixture resembles breadcrumbs, then stir in 2 teaspoons finely grated orange rind, 150 g (5 oz) dried mixed fruit and 125 g (4 oz) caster sugar. Add 1 large beaten egg and 1 egg yolk, plus 1–2 tablespoons milk to bind to a soft dough. Arrange 8–10 mounds of the mixture on a baking tray lined with baking paper and sprinkle with caster, granulated or demerara sugar. Bake in a preheated oven, 190°C (375°F), Gas Mark 5, for 20 minutes or until firm and golden. Cool on wire racks.

Vanilla and Raspberry Fairy Cakes

Serves 4–6

125 g (4 oz) butter or margarine, softened
125 g (4 oz) self-raising flour
125 g (4 oz) caster sugar
2 eggs
1 teaspoon vanilla extract
12 teaspoons raspberry jam, to serve

- In a bowl, beat together the butter, flour, sugar, eggs and vanilla extract until really smooth, pale and creamy. Divide the batter between the greased or paper case-lined cups of a 12-cup muffin tin.

- Bake in a preheated oven, 190°C (350°F), Gas Mark 5, for 12–14 minutes until risen, pale golden in colour and firm to the touch – a wooden cocktail stick inserted into the cakes should come out clean.

- Cool on a wire rack and serve each cake topped with a teaspoon of raspberry jam.

Vanilla and Raspberry Sponge Trifle

Slice 1 raspberry Swiss roll and arrange over the base of a large trifle dish or glass bowl. Stir 1 teaspoon vanilla extract into 3 tablespoons cassis, peach schnapps or cranberry juice and drizzle the mixture over the sponge base. Pour the contents of a 410 g (13¹/₃ oz) can black cherry filling over the sponge, followed by 300 g (10 oz) thick custard. Shake a pressurised canister of fresh dairy cream and squirt several dollops onto the top of the trifle. Serve sprinkled with chocolate curls or a few fresh raspberries.

Vanilla and Raspberry Jam Sponge Cake

In a large bowl, beat 3 eggs and 1 teaspoon vanilla extract with 175 g (6 oz) each of caster sugar, self-raising flour and softened butter or margarine until pale and creamy. Divide the mixture between 2 x 20 cm (8 inch) base-lined cake tins. Bake in a preheated oven, 190°C (350°F), Gas Mark 5, for about 20 minutes until risen and golden. Remove from the tins, peel away the paper and cool on a wire rack before sandwiching together using 4–5 tablespoons raspberry or blackcurrant jam, or your favourite jam. Dredge the top with a sprinkling of caster or granulated sugar and serve as fresh as possible, cut into wedges.

Golden Pineapple with Rice Pudding

Serves 4–6

25 g (1 oz) butter

2 tablespoons demerara or granulated sugar

425 g (14 oz) can pineapple rings in juice, drained

warm or chilled rice pudding, to serve

- To caramelize the pineapple, melt the butter in a large frying pan and sprinkle the sugar over both sides of the pineapple rings to coat. Add the pineapple rings to the pan and fry gently for 2–3 minutes on each side until sticky and golden.

- Cool slightly, then serve with dollops of warm or chilled rice pudding.

Pineapple Baked Rice Pudding

Spoon 2 x 400 g (13 oz) cans rice pudding into a buttered ovenproof dish. Scatter over a 425 g (14 oz) can pineapple chunks in juice, drained. Sprinkle with 2 tablespoons demerara sugar and bake in a preheated oven, 180°C (350°F), Gas Mark 4, for 10–15 minutes until bubbling. Serve warm with ice cream, if desired.

Coconut Rice Pudding with Pineapple

Place 125 g (4 oz) pudding rice in a saucepan with a 400 ml (14 fl oz) can coconut milk, 400 ml (14 fl oz) milk, 50 g (2 oz) light soft brown sugar and 25 g (1 oz) butter. Place over the heat and bring to the boil, then reduce the heat and simmer for about 25 minutes, stirring frequently, until the rice is creamy and tender. Meanwhile, caramelize the pineapple as above. Spoon the coconut rice pudding into bowls and serve with the golden pineapple.

30 Chocolate Orange Cheesecake

Serves 6

250 g (8 oz) dark chocolate
   digestives, crushed
100 g (3½ oz) butter, melted
300 g (10 oz) cream cheese
   or mascarpone cheese
3 tablespoons plain chocolate
   spread
2 teaspoons finely grated
   orange rind
75 g (3 oz) caster sugar
grated orange-flavoured
   chocolate, to decorate

- Combine the crushed biscuits with the melted butter and mix really well to coat. Press the mixture into a clingfilm lined 23 cm (9 inch) tart or cake tin and chill in the freezer or refrigerator while you are making the filling.

- Beat the cream cheese or mascarpone cheese with the chocolate spread, orange rind and caster sugar until thick and smooth. Spoon over the biscuit base and smooth down evenly. Return to the freezer or refrigerator for at least 20 minutes or until required, then remove and decorate with grated orange-flavoured chocolate to serve.

 Chocolate Orange Milkshake

Place 4 scoops of dark chocolate ice cream in the jug of a blender with 750 ml (1¼ pints) milk, 2 tablespoons plain chocolate spread and 1 teaspoon orange extract. Blend until smooth and pour into 3 tall glasses. Repeat to serve 6.

 Chocolate Orange Pots

In a bowl, beat together 200 g (7 oz) cream cheese or mascarpone cheese, 2 teaspoons finely grated orange rind, 125 g (4 oz) Greek yogurt and 3 tablespoons caster sugar until smooth and thick. Stir in 75 g (3 oz) finely chopped dark chocolate and spoon into 6 glass serving dishes. Chill for at least 10 minutes. Meanwhile, mix 175 g (6 oz) crushed dark chocolate digestives with 50 g (2 oz) melted butter. Spoon the biscuit crumbs over the chocolate orange pots to serve.

STU-SWEE-POC

1 ▶ White Chocolate and Apricot Waffles

Serves 4

300 ml (½ pint) single cream
200 g (7 oz) white chocolate
8 sweet toasting waffles
410–420 g (13⅓–13¾ oz)
   can apricot halves in juice
   or syrup, drained and sliced
pistachio nuts, crushed (optional)

- Pour the cream into a small saucepan and heat until hot, but not boiling. Meanwhile, finely chop or coarsely grate the white chocolate and place it in a heatproof bowl. Pour the hot cream over the chocolate and stir until the chocolate has melted and the mixture is smooth.

- Toast the sweet waffles according to the packet instructions and arrange on serving dishes. Drizzle over a little cream and top with slices of apricot. Scatter over a few crushed pistachio nuts to decorate, if using, and serve with extra chocolate sauce.

2 Poached Apricots

Cut 8 apricots in half and remove their stones. Place in a pan with 200 ml (7 fl oz) water, 200 ml (7 fl oz) apple juice, 1 teaspoon vanilla extract (optional) and 2 tablespoons honey. Bring to the boil, then reduce the heat and simmer gently for 8–10 minutes until tender. Pour into a large, shallow bowl and set aside to cool slightly. Meanwhile, make up the white chocolate sauce as above. Serve the poached apricots in attractive glass serving dishes, drizzled with the white chocolate sauce, if desired.

3 White Chocolate and Apricot

Muffins Place 100 g (3½ oz) caster sugar in a large bowl with 225 g (7½ oz) plain flour, 2 teaspoons baking powder, 75 g (3 oz) white chocolate chunks and 50 g (2 oz) chopped ready-to-eat dried apricots. In a separate bowl, beat 2 eggs with 50 g (2 oz) melted butter and 125 ml (4 fl oz) buttermilk or natural yogurt. Pour this mixture into the dry ingredients and mix until barely combined. Divide the muffin mixture between the greased or paper case-lined cups of a 12-cup muffin tin and bake in a preheated oven, 180°C (350°F), Gas Mark 4, for 18–22 minutes until risen and firm to the touch. Transfer to wire racks to cool and serve warm.

10 Berry-Full Baskets

Serves 6

250 g (8 oz) mascarpone cheese
150 ml (¼ pint) double cream
2 tablespoons caster sugar
1 teaspoon vanilla extract
  (optional)
6 brandy snap baskets
500 g (1 lb) mixed summer
  berries (such as hulled
  strawberries, raspberries
  and blueberries)

- Beat together the mascarpone cheese, cream, caster sugar and vanilla, if using, until smooth and thick.

- Spoon into the brandy baskets and top with the mixed berries so that they are tumbling out. Serve immediately.

---

2 Very Berry Tarts

Unroll a 320 g (10¾ oz) sheet of sweet shortcrust pastry and use an 8 cm (3½ inch) plain or fluted pastry cutter to cut out 18 circles. Push into 18 bun moulds and fill each one with 1 teaspoon mixed berry jam. Bake in preheated oven, 200°C (400°F), Gas mark 6, for about 12 minutes or until crisp and golden. Cool on a wire rack.

3 Berry Good Crumble

Mix a 500 g (1 lb) bag of frozen berries with 2 tablespoons light soft brown sugar and tip into a buttered ovenproof dish. In a bowl, combine 75 g (3 oz) each of plain flour and softened butter and rub with your fingertips until the mixture resembles breadcrumbs. Stir in 75 g (3 oz) rolled oats and a small handful of flaked almonds (optional). Tip the crumble mixture over the fruit and bake in a preheated oven, 180°C (350°F), Gas Mark 4, for about 20 minutes or until the topping is pale golden colour. Serve with cream or ice cream, if desired.

30 Chocolate Bar Brownie Buns

Serves 4–6

200 g (7 oz) dark chocolate
125 g (4 oz) butter
2 large eggs
125 g (4 oz) light soft brown sugar
75 g (3 oz) self-raising flour
75 g (3 oz) Mars Bar or other
   chocolate bar, cut into 12 slices

- Melt the dark chocolate with the butter in a small pan set over a very low heat until just melted.

- Meanwhile, whisk the eggs in a bowl with the sugar, then stir in the flour. Pour in the melted chocolate mixture and stir to combine. Divide the mixture between the greased or paper case-lined cups of a 12-cup muffin tin. Push a slice of chocolate bar onto each bun and bake in a preheated oven, 180°C (350°F), Gas Mark 4, for about 18 minutes or until almost firm to the touch. Cool in the tin until firm enough to handle. Serve warm or cold.

 Chocolate Bar Fondue

Place 200 ml (7 fl oz) double cream and 125 g (4 oz) each of chopped Mars Bar and dark chocolate in a bowl set over a pan of simmering water, stirring occasionally, until the chocolate has just melted. Pour into a small fondue pot set over a lit base following manufacturer's instructions, then serve with a selection of sweet dippers, such as strawberries, chunks of banana and marshmallows. (Alternatively, place the pan of water with the melted fondue bowl sitting on top directly onto a heatproof mat in the middle of the table.)

 Milk Chocolate Chip Cookies

Beat 125 g (4 oz) softened butter with 75 g (3 oz) caster sugar until pale and creamy. Beat in 1 egg yolk, then stir in 125 g (4 oz) plain flour, 1 tablespoon cocoa powder, ½ teaspoon baking powder and 100 g (3½ oz) milk chocolate chunks until combined. Use your hands or 2 spoons to place slightly 16–20 flattened balls of the mixture on 2 baking trays lined with baking paper and bake in a preheated oven, 180°C (350°F), Gas Mark 4, for about 12 minutes until slightly darker around the edges. Cool on wire racks.

Chewy Oat and Raisin Bars

Serves 6–8

200 g (7 oz) butter

75 g (3 oz) golden syrup or clear honey

150 g (5 oz) sweetened condensed milk

125 g (4 oz) granulated sugar

325 g (11 oz) rolled oats

75 g (3 oz) raisins

75 g (3 oz) self-raising flour

- Melt the butter with the golden syrup, condensed milk and sugar in a large pan set over a medium-low heat, then remove from the heat and stir in the oats, raisins and flour. Stir well.

- Scrape the mixture into a greased and base-lined baking tin measuring about 25 x 25 cm (10 x 10 inches), with a depth of about 3.5 cm (1½ inches). Bake in a preheated oven, 180°C (350°F), Gas Mark 4, for 15–18 minutes until pale golden in colour.

- Remove from the oven and cool in the tin for 2–3 minutes before marking out and cutting about 16 squares or bars. Allow to cool for about 5 minutes or until cool and firm enough to handle, then transfer to a wire rack.

---

1 **Crunchy Strawberry, Oat and Raisin Fool** Drop 1 tablespoon strawberry jam into the bottom of each of 6 glass serving dishes or ramekins. Mix 300 g (10 oz) strawberry yogurt with 300 g (10 oz) crème fraîche and spoon over the jam. Scatter a small handful of crunchy oat and raisin granola cereal over the top and serve immediately while the granola is still crunchy.

2 **Coconut and Raisin Oat Cookies** In a bowl, beat together 100 g (3½ oz) caster sugar and 100 g (3½ oz) butter until creamy, then add 2 tablespoons golden syrup, 1 small egg, 100 g (3½ oz) plain flour, ½ teaspoon baking powder, 75 g (3 oz) rolled oats, 75 g (3 oz) raisins and 50 g (2 oz) desiccated coconut and mix until combined. Use 2 spoons to arrange about 20 slightly flattened spoonfuls of the mixture on 2 baking trays lined with baking paper. Cook in a preheated oven, 180°C (350°F), Gas Mark 4, for about 12 minutes until golden. Remove from the oven and transfer to wire racks to cool.

Stewed Rhubarb with Custard

Serves 4–6

750 g (1½ lb) rhubarb, cut into
   3.5 cm (1½ inch) lengths
3 tablespoons orange juice
   or water
½ teaspoon ground ginger
   (optional)
50–100 g (2–3½ oz) caster sugar
2 tablespoons custard powder
600 ml (1 pint) milk

- Place the rhubarb in a large pan with the orange juice or water and ground ginger, if using. Reserve 1 tablespoon of the sugar and add as much of the remaining sugar as you like, depending on sweetness desired, to the rhubarb. Heat the pan until the sugar has dissolved, then simmer gently, stirring occasionally, for 6–8 minutes until the rhubarb is tender. Remove from the heat and set aside to cool slightly.

- Meanwhile, place the custard powder in a bowl with the reserved sugar, then add 2 tablespoons of the milk and stir until it forms a paste. Heat the remaining milk in a pan until almost boiling then pour into the paste, in a steady stream, stirring constantly to prevent lumps from forming. Return to the pan and bring to boiling point, stirring constantly, until thickened. (Alternatively, heat 600 ml/1 pint ready-made custard according to the packet instructions.)

- Spoon the rhubarb into bowls and serve with the custard.

 Rhubarb and Custard Sponge Tart Beat 300 ml (½ pint) thick chilled custard into 125 g (4 oz) mascarpone cheese and 1 teaspoon vanilla bean paste or extract (optional) and spread thickly over a ready-made large sponge base. Drain a 539–560 g (1 lb 1½ oz–1 lb 2½ oz) can rhubarb (you need 400 g/13 oz drained rhubarb) and scatter the rhubarb over the sponge. Cut into slices to serve.

 Roasted Rhubarb Crunch Chop 500 g (1 lb) rhubarb into 3.5 cm (1½ inch) lengths and mix in a large bowl with 50 g (2 oz) light soft brown sugar, the finely grated rind and juice of 1 small orange and ½ teaspoon ground ginger. Tip into a large buttered ovenproof dish and cook in a preheated oven, 190°C (375°F), Gas Mark 5, for 15–20 minutes until softened. Remove from the oven and set aside to cool slightly. Meanwhile, beat 125 g (4 oz) mascarpone cheese into 300 ml (½ pint) thick chilled custard and 1 teaspoon vanilla bean paste or extract (optional). Place 8 ginger nut biscuits in a small freezer bag and tap with a rolling pin to break into coarse crumbs. Spoon the roasted rhubarb into dishes, top with a dollop of the mascarpone custard and sprinkle over the crunchy biscuit crumbs to serve.

3 ‹ Frozen Fruit Pudding

Serves 4–6

500 g (1 lb) mixed frozen fruit
175 g (6 oz) caster sugar
125 g (4 oz) butter or margarine,
  softened
2 eggs
125 g (4 oz) self-raising flour
vanilla ice cream, to serve
  (optional)

- Tip the frozen fruits into a buttered 20 x 25 cm (8 x 10 inch) shallow ovenproof dish with 50 g (2 oz) of the sugar.

- Place the remaining sugar, butter or margarine, eggs and flour in a bowl and beat together until smooth. Spoon the mixture over the frozen fruits and smooth down evenly. Bake in a preheated oven, 200°C (400°F), Gas Mark 6, for 20–25 minutes until risen and golden, then serve in bowls with vanilla ice cream, if desired.

1 ‹ Frozen Fruit Sponge Slice

Tip 500 g (1 lb) frozen fruit into a pan with 50 g (2 oz) caster sugar and warm over a medium-low heat for 5–7 minutes, stirring occasionally, until the sugar has dissolved and the warm fruits begin to collapse. Meanwhile, cut a sponge flan base into 4–6 slices and arrange on serving plates. Spoon the warmed fruits over the sponge slices and serve immediately with a dollop of lightly whipped cream.

2 ‹ Frozen Fruit Cakes

In a bowl, beat together 125 g (4 oz) each of margarine and caster sugar, 150 g (5 oz) self-raising flour, 1 teaspoon baking powder and 2 eggs until smooth. Gently fold 100 g (3½ oz) frozen fruit into the batter, then spoon into the greased or paper case-lined cups of a 12-cup muffin tin. Bake in a preheated oven, 200°C (400°F), Gas Mark 6, for 12–14 minutes until risen and pale golden. Serve warm with whipped cream or ice cream.

 # Chocolate Buttermilk Pancakes

Serves 4–6

175 g (6 oz) self-raising flour, sifted
1 teaspoon baking powder
25 g (1 oz) caster sugar
1 egg, lightly beaten
225 ml (7½ fl oz) buttermilk
75 g (3 oz) chocolate chips
butter, for cooking

To serve

whipped cream or ice cream
warm chocolate sauce (optional)

- Combine the flour in a bowl with the baking powder and sugar. Mix the egg into the buttermilk and pour the mixture into the dry ingredients. Beat together until you have a smooth, thick batter, then stir in the chocolate chips.

- Melt a small knob of butter in a large non-stick frying pan and pour large tablespoonfuls of the batter into the pan. Cook gently for 1–2 minutes until bubbles begin to appear on the surface of the pancake, then carefully turn over and cook for about 1 more minute, until golden.

- Repeat with remaining batter, adding a little extra butter, if necessary.

- Serve with whipped cream or scoops of ice cream, drizzled with warmed chocolate sauce, if desired.

 Hot Chocolate Custard Brownies

Pour 500 ml (17 fl oz) ready-made custard into a small saucepan and warm gently until hot, but not boiling. Remove from the heat and stir in 75 g (3 oz) chopped dark chocolate or dark chocolate chips until melted. Meanwhile, arrange 4 chocolate brownies on serving dishes. Pour over the hot chocolate custard to serve.

 Saucy Chocolate Pudding

In a large bowl, beat 100 g (3½ oz) softened butter with 100 g (3¼ oz) caster sugar, 150 g (5 oz) self-raising flour, 3 tablespoons cocoa powder, 125 ml (4 fl oz) milk and 2 eggs until well combined. Scrape into a buttered ovenproof dish. Mix together 50 g (2 oz) caster sugar, 1 tablespoon cocoa powder and 125 ml (4 fl oz) boiling water, then pour this mixture slowly over the batter in the dish. Bake in a preheated oven, 180°C (350°F), Gas Mark 4, for 18–20 minutes until just firm to the touch. Serve with ice cream, if desired.

20 Apricot and Almond Tartlets

Serves 6

1 egg

50 g (2 oz) caster sugar

50 g (2 oz) butter, softened

50 g (2 oz) ground almonds

6 x 8 cm (3¼ inch) baked sweet
   pastry tartlet cases

6 apricot halves in juice, drained
   and sliced

2 tablespoons flaked almonds

ice cream or whipped cream,
   to serve (optional)

- In a bowl, beat the egg with the sugar, butter and ground almonds until smooth and creamy. Divide the mixture between the pastry cases and top with the apricot slices.

- Scatter over the flaked almonds and bake in a preheated oven, 180°C (350°F), Gas Mark 4, for 12–15 minutes until golden. Serve warm with a scoop of ice cream or a dollop of softly whipped cream, if desired.

 Apricot and Amaretti Crumbles

Drain 2 x 410–420 g (13¹/₃–13¾ oz) cans apricot halves in juice and mash with a fork until smooth. Spoon the mixture into 6 glass tumblers. Whip 200 ml (7 fl oz) whipping cream to soft peaks with 1 teaspoon vanilla extract (optional) and 2 tablespoons sifted icing sugar. Spoon over the apricot purée, then crumble 3–4 amaretti biscuits over each one and serve immediately.

 Storecupboard Apricot and Almond Crumble Drain 2 x 410–420 g (13¹/₃–13¾ oz) cans apricot halves in juice, reserving the juice. Roughly slice the apricots and tip into an ovenproof dish with 2 tablespoons of the reserved juice. Mix 50 g (2 oz) chopped almonds into a 225 g (7½ oz) packet of crumble mix and scatter over the apricots. Bake in a preheated oven, 180°C (350°F), Gas Mark 4, for 20–25 minutes until golden. Serve with ice cream.

Ice Cream with Rum and Raisin Syrup

Serves 2

25 g (1 oz) butter
50 g (2 oz) light soft brown sugar
2 tablespoons double cream
1 tablespoon dark rum
small handful of raisins
4 scoops of vanilla or rum and
  raisin ice cream, to serve

- Melt the butter in a small pan with the sugar and cream, stirring until dissolved. Add the rum and raisins, bring to the boil, then remove from the heat and set aside for the raisins to plump up and the sauce to cool slightly.

- Meanwhile, place 2 scoops of ice cream into bowls. Drizzle over the warm rum and raisin sauce to serve.

Rum, Raisin and Pear Trifle

Heat 2 tablespoons coconut-flavoured rum (such as Malibu) in a small pan with a small handful of raisins. Simmer gently for 1 minute, then remove from the heat and set aside for the raisins to plump up. Meanwhile, divide 6 sponge fingers between 2 glass serving bowls. Drain a 410–420 g (13⅓–13¾ oz) can pear halves in syrup or juice, reserving 2 tablespoons of the juice. Stir 2 tablespoons rum into the reserved juice and drizzle the mixture over the sponge fingers. Thickly slice the pear halves and layer over the sponge. Beat 150 g (5 oz) Greek honey yogurt into 125 g (4 oz) mascarpone cheese until smooth and thick, then spoon the mixture over the sliced pears. Scatter over the soaked raisins to serve.

Rum and Raisin Crêpes with

Ice Cream Sift 75 g (3 oz) plain flour into a bowl with 1 tablespoon caster sugar, creating a well or dip in the middle. Whisk 1 egg into 200 ml (7 fl oz) milk, then pour into the well and whisk to incorporate the flour from the edges until the mixture is smooth. Set aside to rest for 10–15 minutes. Meanwhile, warm 3 tablespoons dark rum with 2 tablespoons caster sugar, a small handful of raisins, 25 g (1 oz) butter and 2 tablespoons water in a small pan set over a medium-low heat. Stir to dissolve the sugar, then simmer gently for 2–3 minutes until syrupy. Remove from the heat and set aside to cool slightly. Melt a small knob of butter in a frying pan and pour enough of the batter into the pan to thinly cover the base, swirling to coat the surface evenly. Cook for 1–2 minutes before carefully flipping over and cooking for a further minute, or until golden and crispy. Remove and keep warm while you repeat the process, adding more butter when necessary, until all the batter has been used. Fold the crêpes and arrange on warmed plates, topped with a scoop of ice cream and drizzled with the rum and raisin syrup.

3❶ Warm Cranberry-Poached Pears

Serves 4–6

1.2 litres (2 pints) cranberry or
  cranberry and apple juice
2 tablespoons clear honey
1 teaspoon vanilla bean paste
  or seeds from 1 vanilla bean
  (optional)
2 teaspoons lime or lemon juice
6 large pears

- Pour the cranberry juice into a large pan with the honey, vanilla paste or seeds, if using, and the lime or lemon juice and heat gently until it almost reaches boiling point.

- Meanwhile, peel and core the pears and cut them into quarters. Add to the pan and simmer gently for about 15 minutes, keeping the pears submerged in the poaching liquid, until tender. Remove from the heat and set aside to cool for about 10 minutes.

- Gently spoon the pears into serving bowls and ladle over some of the poaching liquid to serve.

 Crunchy Pear and Cranberry Pots

Place 75 g (3 oz) rolled oats in a bowl with 50 g (2 oz) chopped nuts, 50 g (2 oz) granulated sugar and 50 g (2 oz) melted butter. Stir well to coat, then tip into a large frying pan and toast for 5–6 minutes, stirring frequently to prevent burning, until golden and crispy. Tip into a shallow bowl to cool slightly, then stir in 50 g (2 oz) dried ready-to-eat cranberries. Arrange 2 drained pear halves in juice in each of 4–6 attractive serving dishes and scatter over the crunchy topping to serve.

 Quick Pear and Cranberry Crumble Place 75 g (3 oz) rolled oats in a bowl with 50 g (2 oz) chopped nuts, 50 g (2 oz) granulated sugar and 50 g (2 oz) melted butter. Stir well to coat, then set aside. Drain 2 x 410 g (13¹⁄₃ oz) cans pear halves in juice, reserving 2 tablespoons of the juice. Dice the pears and tip into a shallow ovenproof dish with 50 g (2 oz) dried cranberries, the reserved juice, 1 tablespoon clear honey and 1 teaspoon vanilla extract (optional). Scatter over the oat topping and bake in a preheated oven, 180°C (350°F), Gas Mark 4, for 12–15 minutes until golden. Serve with ice cream, if desired.

30 Lemon Popping Candy Cakes

Serves 6

125 g (4 oz) butter, softened
125 g (4 oz) caster sugar
125 g (4 oz) self-raising flour
2 eggs
1 tablespoon milk
2 teaspoons finely grated
   lemon rind
150 g (5 oz) icing sugar, sifted
2 teaspoons lemon juice
popping candy, to sprinkle

- In a large bowl, beat together the butter, sugar, flour, eggs, milk and 1 teaspoon of the lemon rind until pale and creamy.

- Divide the mixture between the greased or paper case-lined cups of a 12-cup muffin tin and bake in a preheated oven, 190°C (375°F), Gas Mark 5, for 12–15 minutes until golden and risen. Cool on a wire rack.

- Meanwhile, mix the icing sugar with the remaining lemon rind and just enough lemon juice to create a very thick, smooth icing. Spread over the cold cupcakes and sprinkle with popping candy to serve.

 Lemon Cupcake Surprise

Whip 150 ml (¼ pint) double or whipping cream to soft peaks with 1 teaspoon lemon rind and 1 tablespoon sifted icing sugar. Slice the tops off 12 shop-bought lemon or vanilla cupcakes and dollop a scant teaspoon lemon curd onto each one. Top the curd with a spoonful of the whipped cream and scatter over a little popping candy, if desired. Replace the lids to serve.

 Lemon Sorbet Cakes

Slice the tops off 6 shop-bought lemon muffins and carefully remove a little of the sponge from the bottom halves so that you can sit a scoop of lemon sorbet inside each one. Replace the tops and return to the freezer for 10 minutes. Meanwhile, gently heat 50 g (2 oz) caster sugar in a small pan with 2 tablespoons water until dissolved, then increase the heat and simmer gently for 2–3 minutes until syrupy. Remove from the heat and stir in 1 tablespoon lemon juice. Remove the muffins from the freezer, then drizzle over the warm syrup and serve sprinkled with popping candy, if desired.

10 Mandarin Eton Mess

Serves 6

500 ml (17 fl oz) double cream

1 teaspoon finely grated orange rind (optional)

75 g (3 oz) ready-made meringues, broken into pieces

2 x 298 g (10 oz) cans mandarin segments in juice, drained

- Whip the cream with the orange rind, if using, in a large bowl until soft peaks form.

- Fold in the meringues and mandarin segments, reserving a little of each to scatter over the tops. Spoon the mixture into bowls or sundae-style glasses and serve scattered with reserved meringue and mandarin.

20 White Chocolate Mandarin Nests

Melt 150 g (5 oz) white chocolate in a bowl set over a pan of barely simmering water, ensuring the bowl does not touch the surface of the water. Once the chocolate has melted, stir until smooth and set aside to cool slightly. Meanwhile, whip 150ml (¼ pint) double cream with 1 teaspoon finely grated lemon rind and divide between 6 meringue nests. Scatter the segments from a 298 g (10 oz) can mandarins, drained, over the filled meringue nests, then use a teaspoon to drizzle over the melted chocolate. Chill in the refrigerator for 4–5 minutes or until the chocolate has hardened, then serve immediately.

30 Upside-Down Mandarin Muffins

Divide half of a 298 g (10 oz) can mandarin segments, drained, between the greased cups of a 12-cup muffin tin. In a large bowl, mix 250 g (8 oz) self-raising flour with 1 teaspoon bicarbonate of soda, 100 g (3½ oz) caster sugar and 1 teaspoon finely grated orange rind. In a jug, beat 1 egg with 75 ml (3 fl oz) vegetable oil and 150 ml (¼ pint) buttermilk, then pour into the bowl and mix gently with the dry ingredients until barely combined. Spoon the muffin mixture into the moulds and bake in a preheated oven, 180°C (350°F), Gas Mark 4, for 18–22 minutes or until risen and firm to the touch. Turn out of the moulds and serve upside-down with pouring cream and the remaining mandarin segments.

1 Vanilla and Banana Yogurt

Serves 4

4 large ripe bananas
1 tablespoon clear honey
seeds from 1 vanilla pod or
   1 teaspoon vanilla bean paste
   or vanilla extract
500 g (1 lb) natural or vanilla
   yogurt, plus extra to serve
   (optional)
fresh blueberries, to serve

- Peel and roughly chop the bananas and place them in a bowl with the honey and vanilla seeds, vanilla bean paste or vanilla extract.

- Mash the bananas until pulpy, then stir in the yogurt.

- Spoon the mixture into cups and serve scattered with fresh blueberries and extra yogurt, if desired.

2 Baked Bananas with Vanilla Cream

Cut a long slit along the length of 4 large unpeeled bananas and drizzle 1 teaspoon clear honey into each one. Dot with 25 g (1 oz) diced butter, then wrap each banana individually in foil and bake in a preheated oven, 200°C (400°F), Gas Mark 5, for about 15 minutes until the flesh is tender and the skin is blackened. Meanwhile, whip 150 ml (¼ pint) double cream with the seeds from 1 vanilla pod or 1 teaspoon vanilla bean paste or vanilla extract. Arrange the baked bananas on dishes and serve with the vanilla cream.

3 Vanilla and Banana Cakes

Beat 1 egg with 100 g (3½ oz) softened butter, 75 g (3 oz) light soft brown sugar, seeds from 1 vanilla pod or 1 teaspoon vanilla bean paste or vanilla extract and 1 mashed ripe banana. Fold in 100 g (3½ oz) self-raising flour and 1 teaspoon baking powder. Spoon into 8 greased or paper case-lined cups of a muffin tin and bake in a preheated oven, 180°C (350°F), Gas Mark 4, for 18–20 minutes until risen and golden. Remove from the oven, turn onto serving dishes and serve warm with custard or pouring cream.

1 Fresh Fruit Salad

Serves 6

1 small, ripe pineapple
1 small, ripe melon
250 g (8 oz) strawberries
150 g (5 oz) seedless grapes
2 tablespoons apple or
  elderflower cordial (optional)

- Cut the skin away from the pineapple, then slice into quarters and remove the hard core. Cut into bite-sized chunks and place in a bowl, reserving any juices.

- Slice the melon in half and use a spoon to remove the seeds. Cut in half again and remove the skin from the flesh. Cut into bite-sized pieces and add to the pineapple, again reserving any juices.

- Add the strawberries and grapes to the prepared fruit, cutting in half if necessary.

- Mix the reserved juices with the cordial, if using, and drizzle over the fruit. Toss very gently to combine, then serve immediately.

---

2 Fruit Salad Tartlets

Brush 50 g (2 oz) melted butter over six 30 x 40 cm (12 x 16 inch) sheets of filo pastry, then fold each sheet in half then in half again and push into each of 6 cups of a muffin tin, folding down the edges to form 6 tartlets. Sprinkle over 2 tablespoons demerara sugar. Bake in a preheated oven, 190°C (375°F), Gas Mark 5, for 8–10 minutes until crisp and golden. Remove and cool on a wire rack. Once cold, spoon 2 tablespoons of chilled thick custard into each tartlet case and divide 400 g (13 oz) prepared mixed fruit chunks (such as strawberries, melon, grapes and pineapple) between the tartlets to serve.

3 Fruit Salad Frozen Yogurt

Tip a 500 g (1 lb) bag of frozen fruit salad into a food processor with 450 g (14½ oz) fruit-flavoured yogurt or natural yogurt and 2–3 tablespoons clear honey. Blend until just smooth and very thick, then scrape into a shallow container and freeze for 25 minutes or until required.

Swiss Roll Cherry Bites

Serves 6

3 tablespoons granulated sugar
375 g (12 oz) sheet of pre-rolled
  puff pastry
4–5 tablespoons cherry jam or
  your favourite jam

- Sprinkle a clean work surface evenly with the granulated sugar and lay the pastry sheet over the sugar, pressing down to coat. Spread the jam in a thin, even layer over the unsugared side of the pastry, then, starting with a long edge, roll up the pastry.

- Cut the pastry into 24 slices, each about 1 cm (½ inch) thick, and arrange on 2 baking trays lined with baking paper. Bake in a preheated oven, 200°C (400°F), Gas Mark 6, for 12–15 minutes or until crisp and golden. Carefully transfer to wire racks to cool slightly before serving.

 Chocolate Cherry Swiss Roll Trifle

Arrange 1 small sliced chocolate Swiss roll or roulade in a trifle or similar glass dish and pour over 400 g (13 oz) cherry fruit filling. Top the cherry fruit filling with 300 g (10 oz) chocolate custard. Softly whip 150 ml (¼ pint) double cream or whipping cream and dollop over the custard. Decorate with grated chocolate or chocolate curls, to serve.

 Cherry Jam Swiss Roll

Line and lightly grease a 33 x 23 cm (13 x 9 inch) Swiss roll tin. Whisk 3 eggs in a bowl with 100 g (3½ oz) caster sugar until pale and thick. Gently fold in 100 g (3½ oz) sifted self-raising flour and pour the mixture into the prepared tin. Bake in a preheated oven 200°C (400°F), Gas Mark 6, for 10–12 minutes until golden and slightly springy to the touch. Meanwhile, lay a large piece of baking paper on a clean tea towel and sprinkle the surface with about 2 tablespoons caster sugar. Turn out the sponge onto the sugared paper, then peel away the lining paper and roll up the sponge tightly, using the tea towel to help. Leave to cool for 5 minutes, then gently unroll it and cool for 2–3 minutes more. Spread over an even layer of black cherry jam, then reroll and cut into slices to serve.

Apple and Ginger Crunch Cream

Serves 4

75 g (3 oz) mixed chopped nuts
1 teaspoon ground ginger
3 tablespoons caster sugar
50 g (2 oz) breadcrumbs
50 g (2 oz) butter, melted
2 x 385 (12½ oz) cans sliced apples, drained
200 ml (7 fl oz) crème fraîche

- Tip the chopped nuts, ginger, sugar and breadcrumbs into a large frying pan with the melted butter and cook over a medium-low heat for 6–7 minutes, stirring constantly, until crisp and golden. Tip onto a large plate to cool.

- Meanwhile, divide the apple slices between 6 glass dishes and top each one with a dollop of crème fraîche. Spoon the crunchy topping over the top to serve.

Apple and Ginger Baked Meringues

Drain 2 x 385 g (12½ oz) cans sliced apples and mix gently with 2 tablespoons soft brown sugar and 1 teaspoon ground ginger. Divide between 4 individual ovenproof dishes or ramekins. Whisk 1 large egg white in a clean bowl until it stands in stiff peaks. Add 50 g (2 oz) caster sugar, a spoonful at a time, whisking constantly. Spoon this mixture over the gingery apples and bake in a preheated oven, 180°C (350°F), Gas Mark 4, for 8–10 minutes until pale golden. Serve immediately.

Classic Ginger Biscuits with Stewed Apple

Melt 100 g (3½ oz) of butter with 125 g (4 oz) golden syrup over a low heat, then set aside. Meanwhile, sift 325 g (11 oz) self-raising flour, 1 teaspoon bicarbonate of soda and 2 teaspoons ground ginger into a large bowl and stir in 150 g (5 oz) demerara sugar. Pour the melted butter mixture into the bowl and mix well to combine, then use your hands to roll the mixture into about 20 balls. Arrange on 2 baking trays lined with baking paper, then flatten slightly and bake in a preheated oven, 180°C (350°F), Gas Mark 4, for 15–18 minutes until golden and the surface is slightly cracked. Meanwhile, place 2 large peeled and sliced cooking apples in a pan with 3 tablespoons soft brown sugar and a small splash of water. Cover and cook gently for about 10 minutes, stirring occasionally, until softened. Transfer the biscuits to a wire rack to cool, then serve with bowls of the stewed apple and a dollop of crème fraîche, if desired. Store any leftover biscuits in an airtight container.

Peachy Cinnamon Cheesecake

Serves 6

250 g (8 oz) digestive biscuits, crushed

1 teaspoon ground cinnamon

125 g (4 oz) butter, melted

400 g (13 oz) cream cheese

120 g (3¾ oz) peach yogurt

100 g (3½ oz) icing sugar, sifted

410–420 g (13⅓–13¾ oz) can peach halves in light syrup, drained and sliced

- In a large bowl, mix the biscuit crumbs with half of the cinnamon and butter until well coated, then press the mixture into a 23 cm (9 inch) tart or cake tin. Chill in the refrigerator until required.

- Meanwhile, place the cream cheese and yogurt in a bowl and beat in the icing sugar and remaining cinnamon until smooth and thick. Spoon the mixture over the biscuit base and smooth down evenly. Return to the refrigerator and chill for at least 20 minutes.

- Cut into wedges and serve with the sliced peaches.

 Peachy Cinnamon Smoothie

Tip the contents of a 410–420 g (13⅓–13¾ oz) can peaches in juice into a jug blender and add ½ teaspoon ground cinnamon, 300 ml (½ pint) chilled orange juice and 2 peeled bananas. Blend until smooth then pour into 3 glasses with ice cubes and repeat to serve 6.

 Cinnamon Pain Perdu with Peaches In a large shallow bowl, whisk together 3 eggs plus 1 egg yolk, 125 g (4 oz) caster sugar, 1 teaspoon ground cinnamon and 300 ml (½ pint) milk. Dip 3 thick slices of brioche or bread into the egg mixture, turning to coat. Melt 50 g (2 oz) butter in a large frying pan and cook the bread for about 2 minutes on each side until golden. Remove the pain perdu from the pan and repeat the process with 3 more slices of brioche. Serve with freshly sliced peaches.

30 Sweet and Sticky Raisin Pudding

Serves 6

6 tablespoons golden syrup
125 g (4 oz) butter, softened
125 g (4 oz) self-raising flour
125 g (4 oz) caster sugar
2 large eggs
1 teaspoon vanilla extract
 (optional)
75 g (3 oz) raisins
pouring cream or custard,
 to serve (optional)

- Pour the golden syrup into a buttered 20 x 25 cm (8 x 10 inch) shallow ovenproof dish.

- Beat the remaining ingredients together until pale and creamy and spoon over the syrup base. Bake in a preheated oven, 200°C (400°F), Gas Mark 6, for 20–25 minutes or until risen and golden.

- Serve with pouring cream or custard, if desired.

1 Sweet and Sticky Raisin Waffles

In a small pan, melt 25 g (1 oz) butter with 6 tablespoons maple syrup or golden syrup and 75 g (3 oz) raisins until warm and melted. Meanwhile, toast 6 sweet toasting waffles until golden and arrange each one on a serving dish. Top with a scoop of vanilla ice cream and drizzle over the sticky raisin syrup, to serve.

2 Sweet and Sticky Apple and Raisin

Tart Unroll a 320 g (10¾ oz) sheet of pre-rolled sweet shortcrust pastry and use it to line a 23 cm (9 inch) tart tin, trimming away excess pastry. Prick the base with a fork, line with baking paper and cover the base with baking beans or uncooked rice. Bake in a preheated oven, 180°C (350°F), Gas Mark 4, for 12 minutes, then remove the parchment and beans and return to the oven for a further 5 minutes or until crisp and pale golden. (Alternatively, use a ready-cooked sweet pastry case.) Meanwhile, peel, core and slice 4 eating apples into thick wedges. Place in a large frying pan with 50 g (2 oz) butter, 50 g (2 oz) raisins, 2 tablespoons maple syrup or golden syrup, ½ teaspoon ground cinnamon (optional) and 1 teaspoon lemon juice and cook gently for about 10 minutes, turning occasionally, until golden and tender. Scrape the apples into the pastry case and serve with vanilla ice cream or pouring cream.

10 Easy Chocolate Sauce for Ice Cream

Serves 6–8

250 g (8 oz) dark chocolate
3 tablespoons golden syrup
25 g (1 oz) butter
100 ml (3½ fl oz) double cream
vanilla ice cream with tinned or
    fresh fruit, to serve (optional)

- Place the chocolate, golden syrup, butter and cream in a small pan set over a very low heat. (Alternatively, place in a bowl set over a pan of barely simmering water so that the bowl does not touch the surface of the water.) Melt the chocolate and butter gently, stirring until the mixture is smooth and glossy.

- Set aside to cool slightly, then serve drizzled over vanilla ice cream and tinned or fresh fruit, if desired.

20 Easy Chocolate Cupcakes

In a large bowl, beat 2 eggs with 125 g (4 oz) each of softened butter, caster sugar and self-raising flour, 1 heaped tablespoon cocoa powder and ½ teaspoon baking powder until pale and creamy. Fold in 100 g (3½ oz) white or milk chocolate chips, then divide the mixture between the greased or paper case-lined cups of a 12-cup muffin tin. Bake in a preheated oven, 190°C (375°F), Gas Mark 5, for 12–14 minutes until risen and golden. Transfer to wire racks to cool slightly before serving.

30 Easy Chocolate Cake

In a large bowl, beat 175 g (6 oz) each of softened butter, caster sugar and self-raising flour, 2 tablespoons sifted cocoa powder, 1 teaspoon baking powder and 3 large eggs until pale and creamy. Divide between 2 x 20 cm (8 inch), greased and base-lined cake tins and bake in a preheated oven, 190°C (375°F), Gas Mark 5, for 20–22 minutes until risen and firm to the touch. Remove from the oven, turn onto cooling racks and peel away the paper lining. Once cold, sandwich together with desired icing and serve in wedges. Alternatively, serve the cake warm with ice cream and drizzled with the easy chocolate sauce.

Index

almonds
apricot and almond crumble 256
apricot and almond tartlets 256
amaretti and almond crumbles 256
anchovies
pasta bake with anchovies 152
pasta with chillies and anchovies 152
wholewheat spaghetti with
tomatoes and anchovies 152
apples
apple and Brie-stuffed pork 194
apple and ginger crunch cream 272
apple and ginger meringues 272
apple and raisin tart 276
apple, Brie and ham melts 194
gammon with apple and Brie 194
ginger biscuits with stewed
apple 272
apricots
apricot and almond crumble 256
apricot and almond tartlets 256
apricot and amaretti crumbles 256
apricot and prune muesli 24
Bircher-style muesli with apricots
and prunes 24
poached apricots 242
porridge with apricots and prunes 24
white chocolate and apricot
muffins 242
white chocolate and apricot
waffles 242
aubergines
spiced aubergine with chickpeas 94

bacon
bacon and cheese omelette 36
bacon and chicken parcels 198
bacon and egg baguette 36
bacon and pesto pasta salad 192
bacon burger and cheesy chips 56
bacon-wrapped pesto chicken 192
bacon, egg and cheese panini 36
bacon, pea and courgette
risotto 150
bacon, tomato and butter bean
salad 110
barbecue bacon bagel 56
lazy pea and bacon noodles 150
one-pot pea and bacon pasta 150
pesto spaghetti with bacon 192

tomato, bacon and butter bean
soup 110
tomato, bacon and butter bean
stew 110
bananas
banana and bran muffins 30
banana and bran porridge 30
banana and jam toasts 30
bananas with vanilla cream 266
banoffee chocolate muffins 232
banoffee chocolate sundaes 232
boozy banana chocolate trifle 232
vanilla and banana cakes 266
vanilla and banana yogurt 266
basil
tomato and basil bruschetta 182
tomato and basil soup 182
tomato and basil spaghetti 182
bean sprouts
beef and bean sprouts with
peanuts 118
beans
bacon, tomato and butter bean
salad 110
bean and parsley pâté 62
bean and parsley patties 62
bean and parsley stew 62
chorizo and bean stew 172
chorizo and beans with penne 172
chorizo'd baked beans 172
chunky spiced bean soup 140
green bean and broccoli bowl 96
green bean and broccoli salad 96
Mexican bean tostada 184
mixed pepper, kidney bean and
spinach salad 90
piri piri sausage and beans 128
red pepper and kidney bean soup 90
red pepper, kidney bean and
spinach stew 90
rice, green bean and broccoli
bowl 96
sardine and bean bake 116
sardine and bean couscous 116
sardine and bean linguine 102
sardine and three-bean salad 102
sardine, bean and potato salad 116
sausage and cheese baked beans 34
spicy bean quesadilla 140
spicy bean tostada 140

spicy brunch quesadillas 38
sweet potato and green bean
curry 218
tomato, bacon and butter bean
soup 110
tomato, bacon and butter bean
stew 110
tuna and olive bean burgers 130
beef
beef and bean sprouts with
peanuts 118
beef and broccoli stir-fry 78
beef and crispy onion burgers 174
beef and onion stew 174
beef and onion wraps 174
beef and potato balti with
spinach 84
beef chow mein with broccoli 78
beef madras burgers with
spinach 84
beef skewers with satay sauce 118
beef with broccoli and brown
rice 78
corned beef and onion bagel 48
corned beef fritters 48
corned beef hash 48
curried beef stir-fry with spinach 84
Mexican beef fajitas 184
Mexican chilli beef burger 184
spicy peanut and beef wrap 118
beetroot
beetroot and mackerel salad 114
beetroot hummus with mackerel 114
beetroot, mackerel and goats'
cheese lentils 114
red cabbage and beetroot
lentils 108
berries
berry good crumble 244
berry-full baskets 244
very berry tarts 244
blueberry and maple smoothie 28
blueberry maple breakfast muffins 28
blueberry maple pancakes 28
bread
bacon and egg baguette 36
bacon, egg and cheese panini 36
baguette pizza with mushrooms
and peppers 190
banana and jam toasts 30

barbecue bacon bagel 56
breaded fish with mushy peas 216
buttery leek and mushrooms on toast 40
cheese and onion croque madame 52
cheese and onion toasted sandwich 52
cheesy tuna rarebit 154
cinnamon pain perdu with peaches 274
corned beef and onion bagel 48
curried cauliflower lentils on toast 148
French onion soup with cheesy croûtons 52
grilled harissa lamb pittas 88
jalapeño turkey burgers 162
jalapeño turkey melt 162
lemony fish pâté on toast 156
margherita pizza 206
oven-baked chorizo pizza 160
piri piri hot dog 128
sage, lemon and turkey ciabatta 98
sausage and cheese rarebit 70
smoked salmon and cream cheese bagel 42
smoked salmon and sweet chilli baguettes 92
stove-top chorizo pizza 160
Thai grilled chicken sandwich 68
tomato and basil bruschetta 182
under-the-grill chorizo pizza 160
broccoli
    beef and broccoli stir-fry 78
    beef chow mein with broccoli 78
    beef with broccoli and brown rice 78
    broccoli and carrot couscous 106
    carrot and broccoli vegetable stir-fry 106
    crunchy baked carrots and broccoli 106
    green bean and broccoli bowl 96
    green bean and broccoli salad 96
    rice, green bean and broccoli bowl 96
bulgar
    steamed bulgar with grilled vegetables 138
    vegetable bulgar pilau 138

butter
    buttery leek and mushrooms on toast 40
    lemon butter fried fish 156
buttermilk chocolate pancakes 254

cabbage
    fruity braised red cabbage 108
    red cabbage and beetroot lentils 108
    red cabbage coleslaw 108
carrots
    baked carrots and broccoli 106
    broccoli and carrot couscous 106
    carrot and broccoli stir-fry 106
    carrot and feta bubble and squeak 66
    carrot and feta potato cakes 66
    feta and parsley dip with carrot sticks 66
cauliflower
    cauliflower, chickpea and spinach curry 148
    creamy cauliflower coleslaw 54
    curried cauliflower lentils on toast 148
    potato and cauliflower soup 54
    potato, cauliflower and spinach curry 148
    quick cauliflower cheese 54
cheese
    apple and Brie-stuffed pork 194
    apple, Brie and ham melts 194
    bacon and cheese omelette 36
    bacon burger and cheesy chips 56
    bacon, egg and cheese panini 36
    beetroot, mackerel and goats' cheese lentils 114
    blue cheese and walnut pasta salad 100
    blue cheese and walnut wholewheat pasta twists 100
    carrot and feta bubble and squeak 66
    carrot and feta potato cakes 66
    cheese and onion croque madame 52
    cheese and onion potato waffles 144

cheese and onion toasted sandwich 52
cheesy tuna puffs 154
cheesy tuna rarebit 154
chicken, ham and cheese parcels 198
chilli corn cheese muffins 46
classic cheese fondue 200
creamy blue cheese fondue 200
creamy fish pie 136
feta and parsley dip with carrot sticks 66
French onion soup with cheesy croûtons 52
garlicky macaroni cheese 170
grilled gammon with apple and Brie 194
grilled tuna and chive melts 58
jalapeño turkey melt 162
margherita pizza 206
margherita salad 206
margherita tart 206
mint, red onion and feta rice salad 158
minted potato, red onion and feta salad 158
minty pea, red onion and feta omelette with salad 158
pepper and cheese couscous 220
pepper and mozzarella salad 220
quick cauliflower cheese 54
quick cheat's fondue 200
roasted peppers with mozzarella and couscous 220
sausage and cheese baked beans 34
sausage and cheese fold-over 70
sausage and cheese rarebit 70
sausage and cheese rolls 70
skint smoked salmon and cream cheese bagel 42
smoked ham, chicken and cheese puff parcels 198
spicy brunch enchiladas 38
wholewheat pasta bake with blue cheese and walnuts 100
cherries
    cherry jam Swiss roll 270
    chocolate cherry Swiss roll trifle 270
    Swiss roll cherry bites 270

chicken
  bacon-wrapped pesto chicken 192
  chicken, cress and egg mayonnaise
    sandwich filler 60
  chicken, cress and onion sandwich
    filler 60
  chicken, ham and cheese parcels 198
  citrus baked chicken 80
  citrus chicken couscous 80
  citrus chicken salad 80
  creamy chicken and mushroom
    pie 44
  creamy chicken and mushroom
    soup 44
  lime and ginger chicken 112
  lime and ginger chicken pot
    noodle 112
  lime and ginger chicken wrap 112
  smoked bacon and chicken
    parcels 198
  smoked ham, chicken and cheese
    puff parcels 198
  soy chicken and rice noodles 146
  soy chicken with rice 146
  soy noodles with chicken 146
  tandoori chicken and cress
    sandwich filler 60
  Thai grilled chicken sandwich 68
chickpeas
  cauliflower, chickpea and spinach
    curry 148
  spiced aubergine with chickpeas 94
  spiced chickpea hummus with
    crudités 94
  spiced vegetable and chickpea
    soup 94
  spicy brunch burritos 38
chilli
  chilli corn cheese muffins 46
  chilli corn fritters 46
  chilli corn muffins 46
  chilli pea and pulse korma 166
  chilli pea pasta 166
  chilli pea soup 166
  jalapeño turkey burgers 162
  jalapeño turkey chilli 162
  jalapeño turkey melt 162
  Mexican chilli beef burger 184
  pasta with chillies and
    anchovies 152

smoked salmon and sweet chilli
    baguettes 92
sweet chilli pork stir-fry 168
sweet chilli salmon fishcakes 92
sweet chilli salmon quesadillas 92
chives
  creamy mushroom and chive
    linguine 214
  creamy mushroom and chive
    risotto 214
  grilled mushrooms with polenta
    and chives 214
  grilled tuna and chive melts 58
  salmon and chive burgers 64
  salmon and chive fishcakes 64
  skint smoked salmon and herb
    tart 42
  smoked salmon and chive
    mayonnaise 64
  tuna and chive rice salad 58
  tuna, chive and potato gratin 58
chocolate
  banoffee chocolate muffins 232
  banoffee chocolate sundaes 232
  boozy banana chocolate trifle 232
  chocolate bar brownie buns 246
  chocolate bar fondue 246
  chocolate buttermilk pancakes 254
  chocolate cherry Swiss roll
    trifle 270
  chocolate custard brownies 254
  chocolate orange cheesecake 240
  chocolate orange milkshake 240
  chocolate orange pots 240
  easy chocolate cakes 278
  easy chocolate cupcakes 278
  easy chocolate sauce 278
  milk chocolate chip cookies 246
  saucy chocolate pudding 254
  white chocolate and apricot
    muffins 242
  white chocolate and apricot
    waffles 242
  white chocolate mandarin
    nests 264
chorizo
  chorizo and bean stew 172
  chorizo and beans with
    penne 172
  chorizo'd baked beans 172

fried rice with tomato and
    chorizo 104
one pot tomato and chorizo
    jambalaya 104
oven-baked chorizo pizza 160
spicy chorizo and tomato pasta 104
stove-top chorizo pizza 160
under-the-grill chorizo pizza 160
cinnamon
  cinnamon pain perdu with
    peaches 274
  peachy cinnamon cheesecake 274
  peachy cinnamon smoothie 274
coconut and raisin oat cookies 248
coconut rice pudding with
    pineapple 238
cooking 10–11
courgettes
  bacon, pea and courgette
    risotto 150
couscous
  broccoli and carrot couscous 106
  citrus chicken couscous 80
  mackerel and pepper couscous 86
  mackerel with peppers and
    couscous 86
  pepper and cheese couscous 220
  roasted peppers with mozzarella
    and couscous 220
  sardine and bean couscous 116
  spiced lamb burgers with
    couscous 186
  spiced lamb kebab with
    couscous 186
  spiced lamb's liver with
    couscous 186
  vegetable couscous 138
cranberries
  cranberry-poached pears 260
  pear and cranberry crumble 260
  pear and cranberry pots 260
cress
  chicken, cress and egg mayonnaise
    sandwich filler 60
  chicken, cress and onion sandwich
    filler 60
  tandoori chicken and cress
    sandwich filler 60
custard
  chocolate custard brownies 254

rhubarb and custard sponge tart 250
stewed rhubarb with custard 250

eggs
bacon and cheese Spanish
omelette 36
bacon and egg baguette 36
bacon, egg and cheese panini 36
leek and mushroom frittata 40
minty pea, red onion and feta
omelette with salad 158
mushroom and egg-fried rice 134
one-pan sausage omelette 212
potato and onion omelette 144
quick baked ham and egg 32
quick ham and egg tortilla 32
quick ham and eggs benedict 32
sausage and egg scramble 34
skint smoked salmon scramble 42

fish
breaded fish with mushy peas 216
creamy fish pie 136
creamy fish with mash 136
grilled fish fingers with peas 216
herby crust fish with mash 216
lemon butter fried fish 156
lemony baked fish parcels 156
lemony fish pâté on toast 156
Thai fishcakes with dipping
sauce 188
Thai red fish curry 188
fruit
fresh fruit salad 268
frozen fruit cakes 252
frozen fruit pudding 252
frozen fruit sponge slice 252
fruit salad frozen yogurt 268
fruit salad tartlets 268
fruity braised red cabbage 108
fruit, dried
dried fruit compote with ice
cream 234
mixed dried fruit rock cakes 234
mixed dried fruit scones 234

gammon with apple and Brie 194
garlic
garlicky macaroni cheese 170
garlicky spaghetti carbonara 170

one-pot garlicky tomato rice 132
quick garlicky tomato lentils 132
spaghetti with garlic and black
pepper 170
tomato and garlic sauce for
pasta 132
ginger
apple and ginger crunch cream 272
apple and ginger meringues 272
ginger biscuits with stewed
apple 272
ginger marinated tofu and
vegetable parcels 222
gingery grilled tofu with
noodles 222
gingery tofu stir-fry 222
lime and ginger chicken 112
lime and ginger chicken pot
noodle 112
granola
great granola 26
honeyed granola pancakes 26
honeyed granola yogurt 26

ham
apple, Brie and ham melts 194
chicken, ham and cheese
parcels 198
quick baked ham and egg 32
quick ham and egg tortilla 32
quick ham and eggs benedict 32
smoked ham, chicken and cheese
puff parcels 198
harissa
grilled harissa lamb pittas 88
grilled harissa lamb skewers 88
harissa lamb koftas with sesame
seeds 88
healthy eating 10–11
herby baked salmon 76
herby crust fish with mash 216
herby pan-fried salmon 76
herby sausages with honey-mustard
dip 142
herby smoked salmon pasta 76
honey-mustard sausage roll 142
honey-mustard sausages with potato
wedges 142
honeyed granola pancakes 26
honeyed granola yogurt 26

horseradish
simple grilled salmon with
horseradish mash 122
hygiene in the kitchen 11

ice cream
dried fruit compote with ice
cream 234
easy chocolate sauce for ice
cream 278
ice cream with rum and raisin
syrup 258
rum and raisin crêpes with ice
cream 258

lamb
grilled harissa lamb pittas 88
grilled harissa lamb skewers 88
harissa lamb koftas with sesame
seeds 88
spiced lamb burgers with
couscous 186
spiced lamb kebab with
couscous 186
spiced lamb's liver with
couscous 186
leeks
buttery leek and mushrooms on
toast 40
leek and mushroom frittata 40
leek and mushroom pasty 40
leek, mustard and onion tart 50
lemons
citrus chicken couscous 80
lemon butter fried fish 156
lemon cupcake surprise 262
lemon popping candy cakes 262
lemon sorbet cakes 262
lemony baked fish parcels 156
lemony fish pâté on toast 156
lemony mackerel spaghetti 202
lemony salmon goujons 122
lemony spinach and mackerel
bake 202
mackerel salad with lemon
dressing 202
sage and lemon baked turkey
steaks 98
sage and lemon stir-fried turkey 98
sage, lemon and turkey ciabatta 98

smoked salmon with lemon
  mayo 122
lentils
  beetroot, mackerel and goats'
    cheese lentils 114
  chilli pea and pulse korma 166
  curried cauliflower lentils on
    toast 148
  green pepper, mackerel and lentil
    curry with spinach 86
  quick garlicky tomato lentils 132
  red cabbage and beetroot lentils 108
lime and ginger chicken bowl 112
lime and ginger chicken pot
  noodle 112
lime and ginger chicken wrap 112

mackerel
  beetroot and grilled mackerel
    salad 114
  beetroot hummus with mackerel 114
  beetroot, mackerel and goats'
    cheese lentils 114
  green pepper, mackerel and lentil
    curry with spinach 86
  lemony mackerel spaghetti 202
  lemony spinach and mackerel
    bake 202
  mackerel and pepper couscous 86
  mackerel salad with lemon
    dressing 202
  mackerel with peppers and
    couscous 86
maple syrup
  blueberry and maple smoothie 28
  blueberry maple breakfast
    muffins 28
  blueberry maple pancakes 28
mayonnaise
  chicken, cress and egg mayonnaise
    sandwich filler 60
  smoked salmon and chive
    mayonnaise 64
  smoked salmon with lemon
    mayo 122
mint, red onion and feta rice salad 158
minted potato, red onion and feta
  salad 158
minty pea, red onion and feta
  omelette with salad 158

mushrooms
  baguette pizza with mushrooms
    and peppers 190
  buttery leek and mushrooms on
    toast 40
  creamy chicken and mushroom
    pie 44
  creamy grilled mushrooms 44
  creamy mushroom and chive
    linguine 214
  creamy mushroom and chive
    risotto 214
  grilled mushrooms with polenta and
    chives 214
  hoi sin baked mushrooms with
    rice 134
  leek and mushroom frittata 40
  leek and mushroom pasty 40
  mushroom and egg-fried rice 134
  mushroom and mixed pepper
    fold-over 190
  mushrooms in black bean sauce 134
  pepper and mushroom
    stroganoff 190
mustard
  honey-mustard sausage roll 142
  honey-mustard sausages with
    potato wedges 142
  leek, mustard and onion tart 50
  mustard and onion melts 50
  mustard and onion tartlets 50

noodles
  bowl of veggie noodles 164
  Chinese-style pork pot
    noodles 208
  gingery grilled tofu with
    noodles 222
  green curry noodle soup 218
  lazy pea and bacon noodles 150
  lime and ginger chicken pot
    noodle 112
  soy chicken and rice noodles 146
  soy noodles with chicken 146
  sweet and sour pork
    noodles 168
  teriyaki salmon noodles 180
  Thai curry noodle soup 68
  veggie noodle salad 164
  veggie soupy noodles 164

oats
  apricot and prune muesli 24
  baked banana and bran porridge 30
  Bircher-style muesli with apricots
    and prunes 24
  chewy oat and raisin bars 248
  coconut and raisin oat cookies 248
  porridge with apricots and
    prunes 24
  strawberry, oat and raisin fool 248
olives
  margherita tart 206
  tuna and olive bean burgers 130
  tuna and olive pasta 130
  tuna and olive salad 130
onions
  beef and crispy onion burgers 174
  beef and onion stew 174
  beef and onion wraps 174
  cheese and onion croque
    madame 52
  cheese and onion potato
    waffles 144
  cheese and onion toasted
    sandwich 52
  chicken, cress and onion sandwich
    filler 60
  corned beef and onion bagel 48
  French onion soup with cheesy
    croûtons 52
  leek, mustard and onion tart 50
  mint, red onion and feta rice
    salad 158
  minted potato, red onion and feta
    salad 158
  minty pea, red onion and feta
    omelette with salad 158
  mustard and onion melts 50
  mustard and onion tartlets 50
  potato and onion omelette 144
  potato and onion pasties 144
oranges
  chocolate orange cheesecake 240
  chocolate orange milkshake 240
  chocolate orange pots 240
  citrus baked chicken 80
  citrus chicken salad 80
  mandarin Eton mess 264
  upside-down mandarin muffins 264
  white chocolate mandarin nests 264

parsley
bean and parsley pâté 62
bean and parsley patties 62
bean and parsley stew 62
feta and parsley dip with carrot
    sticks 66
pasta
blue cheese and walnut pasta
    salad 100
blue cheese and walnut
    wholewheat pasta twists 100
chorizo and beans with penne 172
creamy mushroom and chive
    linguine 214
creamy prawn spaghetti 136
crispy bacon and pesto pasta
    salad 192
fisherman's sardine linguine 226
garlicky macaroni cheese 170
garlicky spaghetti carbonara 170
herby smoked salmon pasta 76
lazy one-pot pea and bacon
    pasta 150
lemony mackerel spaghetti 202
pasta bake with anchovies 152
pasta with chillies and anchovies 152
pesto spaghetti with bacon 192
poor man's pesto pasta bake 196
poor man's pesto pasta salad 196
poor man's pesto with penne 196
sardine and bean linguine 102
spaghetti and meatballs with spicy
    tomato sauce 120
spaghetti with garlic and black
    pepper 170
spicy chorizo and tomato pasta 104
tomato and basil spaghetti 182
tomato and garlic sauce for
    pasta 132
tuna and olive pasta 130
vegetable pasta bake 82
vegetable pasta bowl 82
vegetable pasta soup 82
wholewheat pasta bake with blue
    cheese and walnuts 100
wholewheat spaghetti with
    tomatoes and anchovies 152
peaches
peachy cinnamon cheesecake 274
peachy cinnamon smoothie 274

peanuts
beef and bean sprouts with
    peanuts 118
spicy peanut and beef wrap 118
pears
crunchy pear and cranberry
    pots 260
quick pear and cranberry
    crumble 260
rum and raisin pear trifle 258
warm cranberry-poached
    pears 260
peas
bacon, pea and courgette
    risotto 150
breaded fish with mushy
    peas 216
chilli pea and pulse korma 166
chilli pea pasta 166
chilli pea soup 166
grilled fish fingers with peas 216
lazy one-pot pea and bacon
    pasta 150
lazy pea and bacon noodles 150
minty pea, red onion and feta
    omelette with salad 158
peppers
baguette pizza with mushrooms
    and peppers 190
green pepper, mackerel and lentil
    curry with spinach 86
grilled pepper and cheese
    couscous 220
mackerel and pepper couscous 86
mackerel with peppers and
    couscous 86
mixed pepper, kidney bean and
    spinach salad 90
mushroom and mixed pepper
    fold-over 190
pepper and mushroom
    stroganoff 190
quick pepper and mozzarella
    salad 220
red pepper and kidney bean
    soup 90
red pepper, kidney bean and
    spinach stew 90
roasted peppers with mozzarella
    and couscous 220

pesto
crispy bacon and pesto pasta
    salad 192
pesto chicken 192
pesto spaghetti with bacon 192
poor man's pesto pasta bake 196
poor man's pesto pasta salad 196
poor man's pesto with penne 196
pineapple
coconut rice pudding with
    pineapple 238
golden pineapple with rice
    pudding 238
pineapple baked rice pudding 238
polenta
grilled mushrooms with polenta
    and chives 214
pork
apple and Brie-stuffed pork 194
barbecue pork strips 56
Chinese-style pork pot noodles 208
pork steaks with corn and rice 208
sticky barbecue pork with
    wedges 208
sweet and sour pork 168
sweet and sour pork noodles 168
sweet chilli pork stir-fry 168
potatoes
bacon burger and cheesy chips 56
beef and potato balti with
    spinach 84
carrot and feta bubble and
    squeak 66
carrot and feta potato cakes 66
cheese and onion potato
    waffles 144
corned beef hash 48
creamy fish with mash 136
fisherman's sardine and potato
    salad 226
herby crust fish with mash 216
honey-mustard sausages with
    potato wedges 142
minted potato, red onion and feta
    salad 158
potato and cauliflower soup 54
potato and onion omelette 144
potato and onion pasties 144
potato, cauliflower and spinach
    curry 148

sardine, bean and potato salad 116
simple grilled salmon with
horseradish mash 122
sticky barbecue pork with
wedges 208
tuna gnocchi bake 154
tuna, chive and potato gratin 58
prawns
aromatic prawn pilau 210
coronation prawn wraps 210
creamy curried prawns 210
creamy fish pie 136
creamy prawn spaghetti 136
Thai prawn curry 188
prunes
apricot and prune muesli 24
Bircher-style muesli with apricots
and prunes 24
porridge with apricots and
prunes 24

raisins
apple and raisin tart 276
coconut and raisin oat
cookies 248
ice cream with rum and raisin
syrup 258
oat and raisin bars 248
raisin pudding 276
raisin waffles 276
rum and raisin crêpes 258
rum and raisin pear trifle 258
strawberry, oat and raisin fool 248
raspberries
vanilla and raspberry fairy cakes 236
vanilla and raspberry jam sponge
cake 236
vanilla and raspberry sponge
trifle 236
rhubarb
rhubarb and custard sponge tart 250
roasted rhubarb crunch 250
stewed rhubarb with custard 250
rice
aromatic prawn pilau 210
bacon, pea and courgette
risotto 150
beef with broccoli and brown rice 78
coconut rice pudding with
pineapple 238

creamy mushroom and chive
risotto 214
curried vegetable and rice bowl 224
fried rice with tomato and
chorizo 104
golden pineapple with rice
pudding 238
hoi sin baked mushrooms with
rice 134
lime and ginger chicken bowl 112
mint, red onion and feta rice
salad 158
mushroom and egg-fried rice 134
one pot tomato and chorizo
jambalaya 104
one-pot garlicky tomato rice 132
pineapple baked rice pudding 238
pork steaks with corn and rice 208
rice, green bean and broccoli
bowl 96
sardine and brown rice bowl 102
soy chicken with rice 146
tandoori turkey steaks with rice 204
Thai curry rice bowl 68
tuna and chive rice salad 58
vegetable curry with rice 224
vegetable rice with curry sauce 224
rum and raisin crêpes with ice
cream 258
rum and raisin pear trifle 258
rum and raisin syrup with ice cream 258

sage and lemon baked turkey
steaks 98
sage and lemon stir-fried turkey 98
sage, lemon and turkey ciabatta 98
salmon
canned salmon and chive
fishcakes 64
fresh salmon and chive burgers 64
herby baked salmon 76
herby pan-fried salmon 76
herby smoked salmon pasta 76
lemony salmon goujons 122
simple grilled salmon with
horseradish mash 122
skint smoked salmon and cream
cheese bagel 42
skint smoked salmon and herb
tart 42

skint smoked salmon scramble 42
smoked salmon and chive
mayonnaise 64
smoked salmon and sweet chilli
baguettes 92
smoked salmon with lemon
mayo 122
sweet chilli salmon fishcakes 92
sweet chilli salmon quesadillas 92
teriyaki baked salmon 180
teriyaki salmon noodles 180
teriyaki salmon skewers 180
sardines
fisherman's pie with sardines 226
fisherman's sardine and potato
salad 226
fisherman's sardine linguine 226
sardine and bean bake 116
sardine and bean couscous 116
sardine and bean linguine 102
sardine and brown rice bowl 102
sardine and three-bean salad 102
sardine, bean and potato salad 116
sausages
grilled sausage and cheese
rarebit 70
herby sausages with honey-
mustard dip 142
honey-mustard sausage roll 142
one-pan sausage casserole 212
one-pan sausage fry-up 34
one-pan sausage omelette 212
one-pan sausage roast 212
piri piri hot dog 128
piri piri sausage and beans 128
piri piri sausage bake 128
sausage and cheese baked beans 34
sausage and cheese fold-over 70
sausage and cheese rolls 70
sausage and egg scramble 34
spaghetti and meatballs with spicy
tomato sauce 120
spicy brunch burritos 38
spicy tomato meatball stew 120
spicy tomato meatball wraps 120
spicy tomato meatballs 120
sesame
harissa lamb koftas with sesame
seeds 88
shopping tips 8

soy chicken and rice noodles 146
soy chicken with rice 146
soy noodles with chicken 146
spinach
    beef and potato balti with
      spinach 84
    beef madras burgers with
      spinach 84
    cauliflower, chickpea and spinach
      curry 148
    curried beef stir-fry with spinach 84
    green pepper, mackerel and lentil
      curry with spinach 86
    lemony spinach and mackerel bake
      202
    mixed pepper, kidney bean and
      spinach salad 90
    potato, cauliflower and spinach
      curry 148
    red pepper, kidney bean and
      spinach stew 90
storecupboard staples 9
strawberries
    crunchy strawberry, oat and raisin
      fool 248
student meals 8
sweet potato and green bean curry 218
sweetcorn
    chilli corn cheese muffins 46
    chilli corn fritters 46
    chilli corn muffins 46
    pork steaks with corn and rice 208

tofu
    ginger marinated tofu and
      vegetable parcels 222
    gingery grilled tofu with
      noodles 222
    gingery tofu stir-fry 222
tomatoes
    bacon, tomato and butter bean
      salad 110
    fried rice with tomato and
      chorizo 104
    garlicky tomato lentils 132
    margherita pizza 206
    margherita salad 206
    margherita tart 206
    one pot tomato and chorizo
      jambalaya 104

one-pot garlicky tomato rice 132
spaghetti and meatballs with spicy
    tomato sauce 120
spicy chorizo and tomato
    pasta 104
spicy tomato meatball stew 120
spicy tomato meatball wraps 120
tomato and basil bruschetta 182
tomato and basil soup 182
tomato and basil spaghetti 182
tomato and garlic sauce for
    pasta 132
tomato, bacon and butter bean
    soup 110
tomato, bacon and butter bean
    stew 110
wholewheat spaghetti with
    tomatoes and anchovies 152
tortilla wraps
    beef and onion wraps 174
    lime and ginger chicken wrap 112
    Mexican bean tostada 184
    Mexican beef fajitas 184
    spicy bean quesadilla 140
    spicy bean tostada 140
    spicy brunch burritos 38
    spicy brunch enchiladas 38
    spicy brunch quesadillas 38
    spicy peanut and beef wrap 118
    spicy tomato meatball wraps 120
    sweet chilli salmon quesadillas 92
tuna
    cheesy tuna puffs 154
    cheesy tuna rarebit 154
    grilled tuna and chive melts 58
    tuna and chive rice salad 58
    tuna and olive bean burgers 130
    tuna and olive pasta 130
    tuna and olive salad 130
    tuna gnocchi bake 154
    tuna, chive and potato gratin 58
turkey
    jalapeño turkey burgers 162
    jalapeño turkey chilli 162
    jalapeño turkey melt 162
    sage and lemon baked turkey
      steaks 98
    sage and lemon stir-fried
      turkey 98
    sage, lemon and turkey ciabatta 98

tandoori turkey steaks with
    rice 204
turkey tikka masala 204
turkey tikka skewers 204

vanilla
    baked bananas with vanilla
      cream 266
    vanilla and banana cakes 266
    vanilla and banana yogurt 266
    vanilla and raspberry fairy cakes 236
    vanilla and raspberry jam sponge
      cake 236
    vanilla and raspberry sponge
      trifle 236
vegetables
    bowl of veggie noodles 164
    curried vegetable and rice bowl 224
    ginger marinated tofu and
      vegetable parcels 222
    green vegetable curry 218
    spiced chickpea hummus with
      crudités 94
    spiced vegetable and chickpea
      soup 94
    steamed bulgar with grilled
      vegetables 138
    vegetable bulgar pilau 138
    vegetable couscous 138
    vegetable curry with rice 224
    vegetable pasta bake 82
    vegetable pasta bowl 82
    vegetable pasta soup 82
    vegetable rice with curry
      sauce 224
    veggie noodle salad 164
    veggie soupy noodles 164

walnuts
    blue cheese and walnut pasta
      salad 100
    blue cheese and walnut
      wholewheat pasta twists 100
    wholewheat pasta bake with blue
      cheese and walnuts 100

yogurt
    fruit salad frozen yogurt 268
    honeyed granola yogurt 26
    vanilla and banana yogurt 266

Acknowledgements

Recipes by: Jo McAuley
Executive Editor: Eleanor Maxfield
Senior Editor: Leanne Bryan
Copy Editor: Salima Hirani
Art Direction: Tracy Killick Art Direction and Design
Original Design Concept: www.gradedesign.com
Designer: Tracy Killick for Tracy Killick Art Direction and Design
Photographer: William Shaw
Home Economist: Joy Skipper
Prop Stylist: Liz Hippisley
Assistant Production Manager: Caroline Alberti